To Don?
Life had it'A po...
regulation and...
make your own.
Guy Muamba

My 51 Opinions:

America Today

by

Guy Muamba

"An opinion is the beginning of Democracy."
GM

ACKNOWLEDGEMENT:

I would like to thank God. For everything. Life, good health, family, friends and my book, it's all because of your grace and goodness, thank you.

Thanking my publishers, l appreciate the opportunity. Thank you so much to Monica Harman, for believing in me since day one (literally day one). Thank you to Marci Clark, my project manager & editor, for delivering a great looking book.

I would like to thank a very special person who helped this project happen a year earlier, my assistant and good friend Mary Lynn Demarco, an Angel sent on earth strictly for me. You are the best, this is only our first project, thank you.

Thanking also another special person. The one who started it all; planting the seed. The seed to one day become a writer. The one who loved us all, instilling great discipline in us and gave us the warmest hugs. The one who used to always tell me that one day l would become a writer. That's my 5th & 6th grade Principal Sister Johanne, at Cathedral Academy in Albany, New York. l love you and thank you, I'm a published writer today.

Thank you to my parents. My father for his intelligence, my mother for the hustle. l love you, God bless you both.

To Dr. Tshisekedi wa Mulumba, for being a great brother and friend to my late father, along with Dr. Kayemba my uncle and another good friend of my father's, thank you for everything.

Finally, thank you to Buckingham Properties, my employer. Thank you to Ken Glazer, Mike Palumbo and Rick Culp. Thanks Mike for your support of this project. To Larry & Jane Glazer, the Glazers, for all you did, thank you, l'm grateful and honored for having the privilege of personally knowing you.

Thank you to all who helped this book come life and to all who will support it, thank you.

This book is dedicated to two very special people. Two male influences. Two people l will forever be linked to; my father and my only child Michael.

My father, for his love, discipline and just sheer intelligence. The smartest man l ever personally knew (Doctorate in Public Administration).Always wishing and pushing for an academic education, thanks Dad. I appreciate everything you've given me. l know you're up there smiling, so am l. May you Rest in Peace.

My son Michael, for the drive. l love you more than you'll ever know and understand. l would give up everything for you and your happiness. l would take the blows, the pain, even the bullet, all for you. Even though you're autistic and may never obtain a Doctorate in Public Administration or write a book on America today, you are responsible for this book, you motivated me, drove me and pushed me every day. lt's not for nothing why you're on the cover. Thank you, son, this one is for you.

Contents

Politics

Sports

Race

Religion

BONUS

Michael Vick's return • Peyton Manning's recovery• Serena Williams' dominance • Lame participation trophies • The gay label • Gay fashion designers • The world is pretty big • Dumb beauty pageants • Howard Stern, Michael Jordan, Clayton Kershaw • The digital age and music • Tom Cruise's no-show • Fast-food • Mark Zuckerberg's genius •Hyundai • Italy • Japan • Germany • Commercials • Polygraphs • My favorites today • 9/11 • Mayor Rudy Giuliani • The Paris attacks • Prisons and education • The rich lifestyle • Blood and love • Comedy and insults • A beautiful woman • Criticizing Valentine's Day • The other ill • The University of Notre Dame • Tickets • The tackiest things • Using the bathroom • Obesity and poverty • Gifts • We human beings • I love New York • Determination

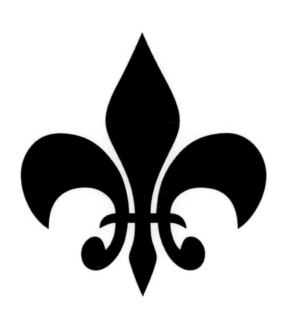

"An opinion is the beginning of Democracy."
GM

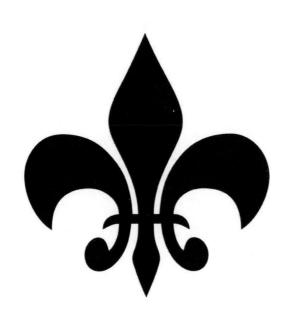

OPENING

This book should not rile anybody up. It should not make anyone angry, for those who disagree with anything they read. This book is simply one man's thoughts, analysis, and opinion on what goes on in America and the world today—no more, no less, an opinion. We all have one; we should. You have to have an opinion on life matters, because you're living; you have a life. If you don't then you're just a rock, a robot. You have to have an opinion to show you have a sense of judging what's right and what's wrong, especially if you have a child and especially if you enter politics. Opinions help us know who is who and what they are about. My senator's opinion is very important to me because it can help me determine if I want this person as my senator. An opinion is the beginning of democracy.

GM

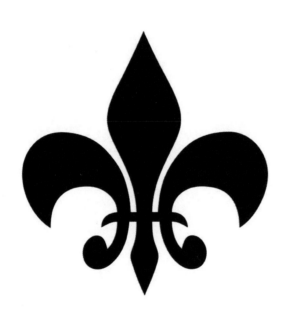

SOCIETY

1. THE INDECENT PROPOSAL

W e've all seen the movie. A very wealthy businessman proposes to a couple to sleep with the wife for a million dollars. In the movie, it's made to look like a business deal.

If a crack fiend is bending over for five dollars in an alley, she's a whore.

If the girl next door on unemployment screws the superintendent of the building for twenty bucks, she's a whore.

If a prostitute spends one night with a millionaire for any amount of money, she's a whore.

However, if the director of personnel (female) sleeps with the CEO for a million bucks in a one-nighter, it's a "business deal." No, it's not!

If a beautiful young lady auditioning for a part sleeps with the film director (or gets offered a million bucks for one night), it's a "business deal." No, it's not.

A lot of women of all walks of life, if asked if they would sleep with a man for a million bucks—a perfect stranger—would say yes in a heartbeat.

My opinion on that? Why is the crack fiend only a whore then? Why just the prostitute? Five or twenty is enough for the crack fiend and the prostitute, for their needs, the girl on unemployment too. A million is just more money. You're all whores, my opinion, like it or not. You are all whores, no difference at all.

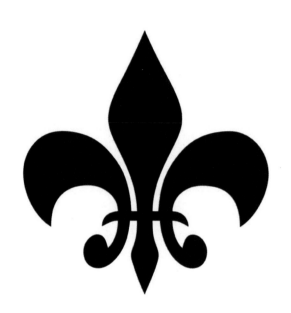

SOCIETY

2. MEN ARE DOGS

We've heard this over and over and over again.

Men are dogs, all men are dogs, all men are the same, all men cheat, they're all the same.

My opinion on that? These men that are all dogs, who are they sleeping with? Animals? Robots? Plants? No, they're sleeping with or screwing women. Women who know that he's married or has a girlfriend. These women who men bang on the side aren't raped or blackmailed into sex, it's consensual. Yes, it's wrong for the men to be dogs, but it is also wrong for the women. They are dogs also, without question.

A lot of women can be worse than men. They will sleep with their sister's boyfriend, mom's boyfriend, best friend's boyfriend. The dude is wrong for that, but so is the woman he's banging. She knows he has a woman. She isn't being raped.

Tiger Woods was dead wrong for all those chicks he was banging while he had a beautiful family. However, it sickened me how they all came out like he raped them. Are you serious? They knew his situation and didn't care.

Yet all men are dogs.

SOCIETY

3. INTERRACIAL COUPLES AND GENERAL ASSUMPTIONS

The general and first thing we think of when we see a white chick who dates a black guy is, "Oh, she likes black guys."

When a white guy comes in a room or is strolling hand in hand with his black wife we think, "Oh, he's got jungle fever. He loves black women."

My opinion on that? The white chick probably dates all races and things happened to work out with the black guy, and they're going forward.

The white guy with the black wife? Same thing. He probably, before marrying his wife, dated all races and the last one things just happened to time out perfectly when he was ready to get married.

I have worked with black girls who didn't like or had an attitude towards another black guy who had a white girl or white wife. His previous relationship could've been a black or Latino girl. Especially with black girls, when they see a black dude with a white girl. "Oh, he likes white girls." Bull crap. He might like white girls only, it's possible, but he also could like all races and things just happened to work out with this one here (white girl), and they're moving on.

My opinion on that? I already said it—bull crap.

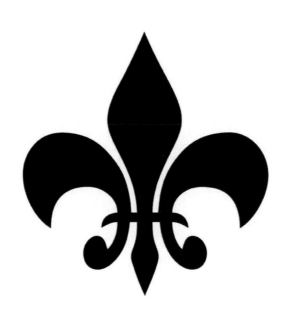

SOCIETY

4. SHOES AND CIGARETTES

A smoker who buys a pack a day at ten bucks spends $3,640 a year on cigarettes. Let's not get into the health issue but just the money—over three grand on cigarettes a year. Some of them smoke weed, which would likely take them into about five grand a year on smoking.

Me? I have never smoked, drank, or gotten high during my whole life. A very good friend of mine, a bartender, would always bark at me and my taste for very expensive shoes. At the time, I would spend about $1,000 to $1,500 a year on nice shoes—$200 to $500 a pair, some even $800. He would tell me to invest my money.

My opinion on that? My buddy never would bark at smokers when they would step out for a cigarette. He wouldn't bark at them for spending $3,600 a year on cigarettes or wouldn't advise them to invest their money. If you smoke cigarettes, to some people it's nothing, it's normal. If you smoke weed, again, it's nothing. It's normal, you're even really cool when you smoke weed. However, cigarettes and weed run you about three to five grand a year (not including alcohol) but if I—who worked three jobs and didn't smoke, drink, or get high—spent $1,500 a year on nice Italian shoes, I'm nuts. I'm crazy. I'm weird. When you're a nicotine addict, you're cool. When you dress nice, you're an idiot. When you spend five grand on cigarettes and weed and alcohol it's okay, you're normal. Fifteen-hundred dollars a year on shoes? You're an idiot. Really?

I love him, though. He's one of the smartest people I have ever known—super smart, knows everything about everything, a real connoisseur.

SOCIETY

5. DEMOCRACY AND PEOPLE

People love democracy. They love their freedom and their liberty.

They love to say what they want, dress how they want, and go where they want which is great.

My opinion on that? Those same people, including me, need to please shut up when someone else says something they don't like, wears something strange, or goes or does stuff we don't do.

We love to criticize. We love to critique. We love to talk about people who don't do or like what we do or what we like. Everybody in the world cannot love blue, or red, or yellow. We are all different. If a black guy loves R&B and hip hop it's okay. If a black guy loves opera or classical or country music (which does happen), there's something wrong.

Democracy starts with you and me. One person, one vote, one voice, one opinion. My adult life—no, my whole life I've been looked at weird because I don't smoke, drink, or get high. As long as someone is not hurting you or anyone else and likes to wear bell-bottoms in 2016, that's his or her choice. If a person listens to a certain genre of music you can't stand, it's his or her choice. Do not insult or criticize him or her. We criticize people every day for their liberty, and yet we scream and demand democracy for all. Yeah, right.

SOCIETY

6. PEOPLE CHEERING OJ

OJ Simpson. Hall of Fame NFL running back. Acquitted for a double homicide.

I remember OJ on the run in his Bronco with his buddy Al Cowlings. I remember people cheering him on. I remember signs that read, "Go, OJ, go!"

My opinion on that? That's the world we live in today. As long as it wasn't my daughter and her boyfriend that OJ allegedly just killed, then NO, HE DIDN'T DO IT.

If it's an average Joe on the run, then nobody's cheering for him to flee, there won't be any signs cheering him to go! Yet we see people in that infamous video cheer OJ like the two victims didn't even matter. If he didn't do it, then go tell your story in court. Only if it happens to us, only when our daughters get killed, raped, or beaten do we stand up against the perps.

If it's an athlete, actor, or singer that we love or that we truly adore, then we think he or she is innocent. Mike Tyson got two years for raping a beauty pageant. If an average Joe that works at Wendy's rapes a beautiful beauty pageant. Believe me, he's not getting two years—five at least.

Judges and juries can be so lenient on celebrities. We just love celebrities. We love to give them free stuff. We'll even give them a pass on justice. I love you, Mike, and not saying you raped her, but you got convicted of rape. An average Joe at Wendy's raping a beauty pageant would never get two years. Never.

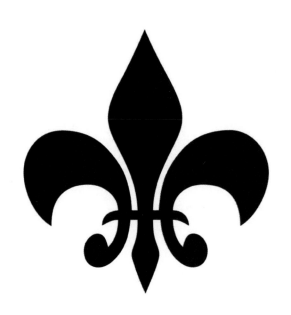

SOCIETY

7. *Negativity dominates positivity*

Negativity makes the world go around. Positivity has become boring.

Do something positive, sensible people will appreciate that and pay attention. Do something negative the whole world will pay attention, the media will love you.

My opinion on that? An actor or athlete can visit or donate huge dough to a certain school and it won't be talked about much, one day that's all. That same actor or athlete can catch a DWI, and it will run for a month, probably longer, in the media. Rasheed Wallace, one of my favorite NBA players of all time, was only known for technical fouls. Yet he gave coats, turkeys, and other good stuff to families in need on Thanksgiving and Christmas. A lot of people don't want to talk about that, and this was genuine of him—not some fake stunt to mask some bad person that he was inside.

If there's a good story about you, about 30 to 50% of the people at your school, job, or neighborhood will know about it. If there's a bad rumor or story about you, 100% of the people at your school, job, or neighborhood will know about it. This negativity really plagued hip hop badly at one time, and I love hip hop. You didn't get signed as a rapper or get any air play if you didn't kill or sell drugs in your songs. Pathetic, absolutely ridiculous. Shout out to A Tribe Called Quest.

SOCIETY

8. RICKY WILLIAMS THE WEED SMOKER

We all remember the whole Ricky Williams saga.

Ricky Williams was a professional running back in the NFL who had trouble playing football because of suspensions by the NFL for weed smoking. At the time, he was made to be this crazy addict, this thug, this irresponsible idiot blowing away his career. TV analysts judged, judged, judged, and judged Ricky for smoking marijuana.

My opinion on that? I don't drink, smoke, or get high—never have my whole life. So now that weed smoking is becoming more and more legal across the U.S., what do the NFL analysts, and TV commentators have to say about that? What do they say to the people smoking weed in Colorado? Not the medicine marijuana, the recreational real thing. What do you say to all these millions and millions of people who smoke weed legally here in the U.S. and in Europe (Amsterdam). Do you call all these people the same names? Do you judge all these people the same way you judged Ricky? Are you going to frown upon all of them the same way? Are they all addicts? Idiots? Thugs? Are they all blowing their lives away, too? I'm not pushing for legalizing weed smoking everywhere here, no, I'm not. The point is, anyone who chewed Ricky up back then is a hypocrite. Stop the hypocrisy and the judging.

SOCIETY

9. THE DRINKING AGE IN AMERICA

In the U.S., you have to be twenty-one to drink. You have to be eighteen to smoke. Twenty-one years old.

My opinion on that? Bull crap. You mean to tell me it's ok for you as a government, to send someone's child overseas at eighteen years of age to legally kill, but they are not able to buy a drink? What planet is this? It is absolutely okay to kill at eighteen, but not have or buy a drink? Absolute bull crap.

Drinking has more of an issue with an eighteen year old than killing? Line up all the politicians and psychologists you want to prove me wrong, and I won't even give them five seconds to hear what they have to say. It's all a bunch of politics, if you raise the enlisting age to serve in combat to twenty-one, then you have less people. If you reduce the drinking age to eighteen then you have now a bunch of teenagers buying and drinking alcohol. Simple as that. I just have a very hard time believing that it's okay to kill at eighteen but not okay to buy a drink. I must've missed something.

A friend of mine's father served in the military. He killed men, women, and children. He had a super hard time with how God allowed him to keep his family but kill others. He's dead now. How can it be okay to subject an eighteen-year-old to that, but not a drink or the purchase of a drink? I'm sorry but I disagree 100% with this age limit. One of the two has to change, drinking or serving in combat.

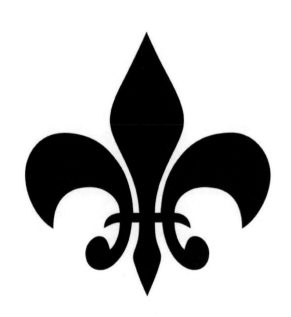

SOCIETY

10. LAWYERS

Lawyers. Bad lawyers. Wow, I don't know what to really say anymore about bad lawyers, meaning lying lawyers.

The way they go in court and support killers and rapists and thieves…and lie, lie, lie, lie, lie.

My opinion on that? How, as a lying lawyer, do you look at yourself in the mirror? How do you look at your friends if you have any in the eye? Do you get mad at your wife for lying that she didn't sleep with your friend while she did? Do you get mad at your kids when they cheat in class? When you lie in court to get your client acquitted with fake alibis and other bogus information, you are orchestrating a scam on the jury. So, do you get upset when someone else scams you in life? Do you care about the victims? The dead? The raped? Do you feel anything at all inside of you? It's just money? Or just winning a case? Lying lawyers are unreal to me. I don't know how they raise their kids honestly. Their spouses are just as guilty. I really don't know how you sleep with someone like that and how you put your kids' upbringing in their hands. You're both guilty and wrong.

POLITICS

1. WISHING FAILURE ON PRESIDENT OBAMA

Some people did just that. I listened to them say, "I wish he fails."
Wow.

Others wished death, hate, and all kinds of bad things on him.

My opinion on that? Hate it or love it, if you live in the U.S., President Obama is your president. Wishing him failure is ridiculous and dumb. When he fails, you fail, the economy fails, gas prices go up, food goes up, the gas and electric bill goes up, college tuition goes up, unemployment goes up, and taxes go up.

I don't agree with everything President Obama proposed and did, but the majority of it I did. An overwhelming majority, probably 80%, agreed and supported him that much. Even if I didn't, I would never wish him failure, hate, or death. If I thought he was wrong about something, I would do something, if I could. If I couldn't, I would pray he changes his mind or some other people to change his mind. You have to remember we don't have a dictatorship in America, we have a two-term democratic presidency with a Senate and a Congress, meaning anything the president proposes, it's voted on first, and then passed into law or policy or given a budget. Another group of people have agreed with his idea or proposal and voted yes. A group of people bigger than the group who disagreed. It's all voted on and, apparently, whatever he does makes a lot more sense to those in charge because they voted yea more than they voted nay. I trusted his judgement years ago when he voted not to go to war in Iraq. The CIA fabricated all these numbers on what Saddam Hussein had and how long before he could build whatever. All along these were lies just to go to war to remove Saddam Hussein from power. George Bush, a lot of American soldiers got killed in Iraq, over something that was not true, I hope you sleep at night.

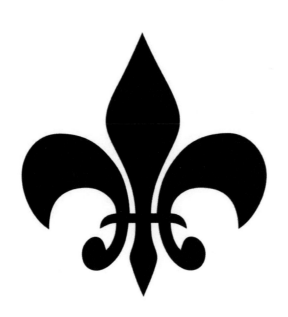

POLITICS

2. POLITICIANS ALWAYS SWITCH

Dick Cheney, Rob Portman, Jon Huntsman, and many more always switch opinions and support when one of their own (a family member) is involved, or when they want to run for the Oval office.

My opinion on that? Especially when it comes to gay marriage, you have to support gay marriage if you are going to run for the presidency because everybody is all for it now. Some politicians do not support anything gay until Susie or Mark, their kid, comes out of the closet. Some do not support stem cell research until a loved one needs the help of that research. A bunch of hypocrites. That is phony and dishonest of them. When you switch like the politicians, you're saying that before you didn't care, but now you only care because your son or daughter needs help or is gay.

I could never trust or vote for a politician again who switches opinions and support only after a loved one is in the mix or if he suddenly decides to run for office. However, politicians are people like you and me, and they can change their minds on any topic. They just can't do it out of politics and personal gain, that's not genuine. Think about it, today I'm opposed to gay marriages, tomorrow my son tells me he's gay and then—boom!—I switch? I don't like that.

POLITICS

3. One country, one Constitution, many rulings

We have one country, one Constitution, but good God do we have the strangest sentences and rulings. Yes, we have fifty different states that see things a little differently than each other, but come on.

My opinion on that? A woman in Texas got ten years of probation for killing her husband. What? She got two days in jail, a $10,000 fine, and ten years of probation. First-degree murder we're talking here! People do time for DUIs and DWIs, and she's out on probation for first-degree murder. Texans are so weird. The jury gives the sentences, too. These jury members, would they recommend the same sentence if it was their brother or sister that was killed?

Their argument? This woman was a very good mother. Pfff, give me a break. Lil Wayne got caught with a gun on his tour bus and got a year. He first pled not guilty, but after DNA evidence on the gun would've been admissible in court, Wayne pled guilty quick or faced three and a half years in jail. So, let me see, one to three and a half years for a gun on a bus in New York State. But ten years of probation for killing your husband. You gotta be kidding me. Same country, same Constitution. I don't care how different the states and their gun laws are or how good a mother can be but first-degree murder and having a gun on a tour bus (that didn't kill anyone) is extreme for differences in sentences.

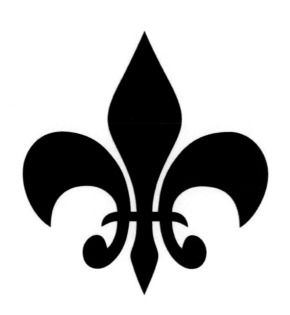

POLITICS

4. *LARGE-SIZED DRINKS AND PORNOGRAPHY*

Former Mayor Michael Bloomberg tried to ban large-sized non-diet sugary drinks from restaurants, fast-food joints, movie theaters, and sports arenas in New York City, citing health concerns.

People, legislators debated this.

They really sat down and debated this! Cut the crap. My diet is my business. How do you know if I work out or not? How do you know what anyone does after a large-sized soft drink? Do you really believe that large-sized drinks in all of these places are the cause of obesity in New York City? That's a joke. So let's get this straight—he cited health concerns, so if the porn business was in New York City instead of California he would outright ban it, right? We all know what goes on in the porn business and that people swallow all kinds of stuff, but it's their right and freedom to do what they want. No one has ever, in these modern and present days, tried to ban pornography. It's not even an issue or a conversation. Yet, you sit around a table and debate what size drink I can have in public places? Really? Not one issue with porn, but with what size soft drink I have? And this is all in the same country, with the same Constitution? How is that possible? For legislators really to allow me to do all kinds of stuff in porn, and then try to check what size Pepsi I get before seeing a game or a movie? Ridiculous! Let people be free please.

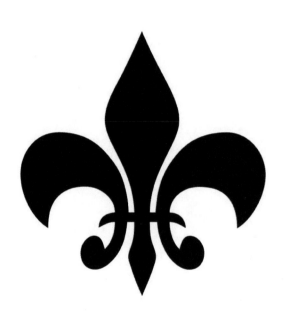

POLITICS

5. CHURCH AND STATE

Church and State. There's supposed to be a fine line.

One cannot override the other.

My opinion on that? Bull crap, I'm a Christian. Easter is for Christians. Christmas is for Christians. Also, we take Easter and replace Jesus with some little bunny? We take Christmas and replace the Lord Jesus Christ with some fat dude in a red suit? All this to separate Church and State. If you want to separate the two, well, create your own Easter and your own Christmas, don't re-arrange or taint ours.

Don't give Easter breaks or Christmas breaks. Take "In God We Trust" off the currency. Take prayer out of all presidential inaugurations. Not one single tax dollar should go to a religious cause. We sing "God Bless America" all the time. There is no separation of Church and State in America. All kids in school are not Christians. Some kids are Muslims, Buddhists, and what have you. Do you give them all their holidays?

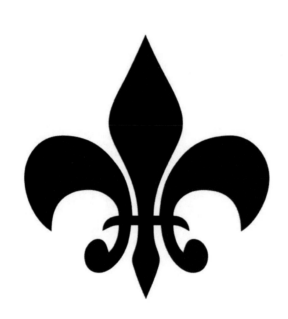

POLITICS

6. SMOKING

The tobacco industry was sued several years back. They were accused of hiding the fact that nicotine smoking was addictive. They were also ordered to pay for certain health costs of the victims.

My opinion on that? Bull crap! Now that we all know that nicotine smoking is addictive have we stopped? No, do people who just started smoking quit because they just found out that nicotine is addictive? No, hell to the no. Are thirteen, fourteen, and fifteen year olds still smoking? Yes.

It's all a big farce to get some money from the tobacco industry. No thirteen-year-old is nicotine addicted. No fourteen-, fifteen-, or sixteen-year-old either.

You have to want to smoke to become addicted. It all begins with teenagers wanting to be cool, look cool, and act cool, and that all begins with a cigarette in the hand or on their lips or on their ear. Insecurity. Yes, insecurity, the number one reason we have smokers worldwide. Teenagers, even adults, want this cool look. They're not secure being themselves. Not smoking and being healthy. They want to look like a gangster, the bad guy in the movies, the boys want to impress the little girls that they are cool, older, and smoke. Pfff. Pathetic. No toddler, no eight-year-old, no twelve-year-old is born nicotine addicted. You start off imitating or wanting to do something others do. Insecurity. You simply can't be you (non-smoker) you want to look like James Dean, so that twenty years later you can sue the tobacco industry. Pffff.

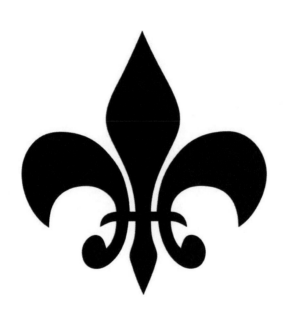

POLITICS

7. CONCUSSIONS

Concussions are a big issue today, in all sports. The NFL is being sued every day for concussion-related issues. Plaintiffs say the NFL hid the dangers of concussions from the general public years ago.

My opinion on that? Bull crap. Now that we all know what these dangers are, people (players) suddenly just quitting football? Is there no more pee wee football? Are high school kids all of a sudden just going to stop playing? Are parents nationwide yanking their kids out of football? So what makes you believe that if the NFL warned the general public about the dangers of concussions years ago, when football started, that people would not have played this game? It's the same as smoking, now that we all know that nicotine is addictive people don't care at all. They're still smoking at thirteen, fourteen, fifteen, and sixteen years old. Same for football. We know the dangers of concussions, but we're still playing. And say what you want—any player killing himself or shooting anybody and people blaming it on football and the repeated blows to the head does not sound true to me. Why? Because non-athletes do the same thing in society, and it's not because of blows to the head. If they kill themselves or others, it's their own personal issues or the whole league would be committing suicide or shooting people.

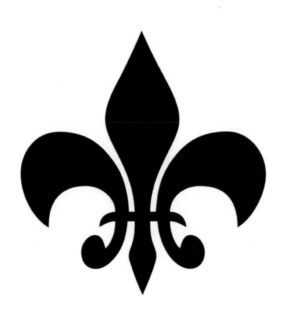

POLITICS

8. THE CONSISTENCY OF ARAB GOVERNMENTS

Arab governments have some very tough laws and strict policies, especially in the Middle East. I disagree with a good portion of them. Especially when it comes to women. They are very restricted to a lot that life and this world has to offer. I do, however, love how they follow through on their judicial system.

My opinion on that? When Saddam Hussein was sentenced to death, he didn't live past thirty days. Meaning when you're sentenced to death, you are going to die. In America, when you get sentenced to death, guess what? You get a cool ten to fifteen years on death row. Pathetic. Eating up taxpayers money while you were supposed to be long gone.

Arabs do what they say they're going to do, period. In the U.S., we sugar coat all sentences. Someone gets twenty years, they will only do nine or ten. The death penalty? Where's the punishment?

If you give out severe punishment and follow through, meaning have the person serve every single day and hour of their time, people would think twice before pulling the trigger or raping that poor woman. If you are sentenced to death for raping and killing some eighty-year-old woman, you have no business living past thirty days of your sentence. Stop wasting taxpayers' money.

POLITICS

9. THE STATE OF AFRICA TODAY

Africa is and always has been at the bottom in terms of development.

Africa is a continent full of a lot of good, but the bad unfortunately far outweighs the good.

With all the minerals and natural resources this continent has, if every penny, every dollar, went where it was supposed to—schools, roads, housing, healthcare, and education—it is very scary to think how developed it would be. Especially the Democratic Republic of Congo, which would be three times what Johannesburg is, in all four corners of the country. Instead, the Congo, one of the richest countries in the world, is also one of the poorest countries in the world.

My opinion on that? It's simple, their presidents and crook-friends destroy these beautiful countries. You have presidents with billions in offshore accounts and in European banks. How do you explain an American president making 400 grand a year and an African president with billions in accounts in other countries? When will the UN do something about the Cayman Islands and Switzerland? These countries are just as guilty for the poverty in Africa as the heartless monsters who are in power.

It's an election year in the Democratic Republic of Congo, please support my uncle and very dear friend of my late father, Dr. Etienne Tshisekedi wa Mulumba, the elected president in 2011, who never took office and power because of fraud and corruption. He is a very, very honorable man and the right leader. May God bless you. He is the first ever Congolese to obtain a doctorate in law.

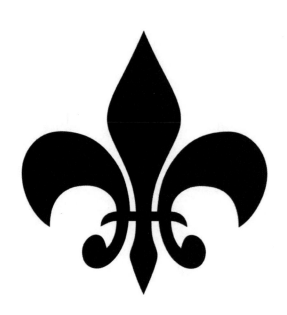

POLITICS

10. THE BIGGEST CRIMINALS

The biggest criminals in the world are not locked up. They go unpunished every day. They feel like they are untouchable. Politicians, priests, pastors, and CEOs. Some of them are really, really bad.

My opinion on that? Some criminals are locked up for crimes against one individual. These monsters commit crimes that affect millions or thousands. Not every single one of them is a criminal. They embezzle money. They take bribes. Politicians favor companies or subjects that can help them and their own stay in office. Dirty priests do harm to children or commit sexual immorality amongst themselves, but when found out, they only get moved around to other churches or parishes—their authorities are just as guilty. Pastors are no different, but like to sleep around with church members, embezzle or steal church designated funds. They love luxury, but it has to be earned, not taken from other people.

Pastors in Africa are the worst. They dupe their members into sleeping with them ridiculously with insane beliefs. CEOs, my goodness, their salaries are sick. When fired, they leave with a gazillion severance package. No matter how their companies are performing, they get ridiculous raises. Even when they have to lay off so many workers, meaning so many families affected. Are they still throwing two million dollar birthday parties for their wives?

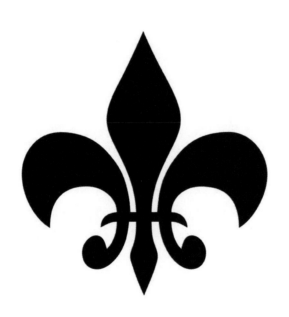

SPORTS

1. FOOTBALL AND SNAPPING THE BALL

In football, teams line up and snap the ball quickly after they see that the previous play was not a completion or could be reversed, to their disadvantage.

Every quarterback, every team does it.

My opinion on that? It's disgusting. It's cheating—plain and simple. How, as a quarterback or a coach, can you sit at home and teach your kids good morals but then get on TV in front of millions and cheat? You know the ball hit the ground and then the receiver caught it, but you rush to huddle up snap so they don't review it? Are you kidding me? It's cheating. Where are your morals? I'm talking to all these QBs, players, and coaches. Where are your morals? What do you say to your kids when they ask you about that? Or do they at all? I don't know about you, but I like to win with a clean and clear conscious. I like to look at a ring or a trophy with pride and have no guilty conscious. I like to feel good about winning without cutting corners. I like to be happy that I beat my opponent fair and square, with no help from the referees, no help from a bad call, no steroids, and no advantage of any sort whatsoever, none. I could never be happy with a win or a championship that was decided by cheating or disadvantage. Never. True winners earn their wins; they don't cut corners, take steroids, or cheat. True winners don't line up and snap the ball quickly.

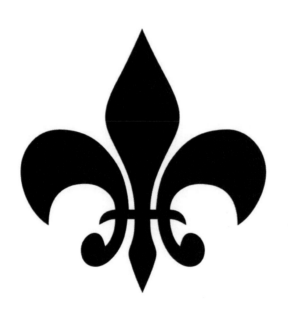

SPORTS

2. PLAYOFFS WAY OVERRATED

Playoffs are good for a team. They give you a chance to win the championship. Only the teams in the playoffs can win a championship, and not the ones who don't make the playoffs.

Some coaches get incentives if their teams make the playoffs.

My opinion on that? In basketball, yes, playoffs are cool, because in the NBA you are guaranteed four more games to play which generates a lot of money for the team and the city, plus a chance to advance to the championship barring you have to face Lebron James (shout out).

In football, no, because it's one and done if you lose. One year my Giants didn't make it and the Redskins made the playoffs. I couldn't hear the end of it from Redskins fans. The following week, in the evening, the Redskins were like me, on the couch watching, meaning one and done. Pfff, really? That's it? The hype of the playoffs? All you got was one more game. You've accomplished something when you make the conference championship or the Big Dance, the Super Bowl. Win at least two games, just making the playoffs is way overrated in football. My Giants got better picks in the draft than the Redskins who made the playoffs, but were home watching like the rest of us the following week. Baseball and basketball playoffs are cool to make, not football.

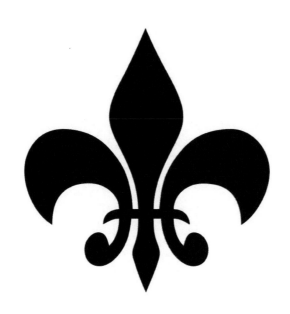

SPORTS

3. *NBA FIGHTING VS. NHL FIGHTING*

Fighting in hockey, they love it. Players and fans.

Some hockey fans don't truly enjoy a game till there's a fight or a brawl.

My opinion on that? It's disgusting how NBA players are characterized when they fight or throw a punch. An NBA player is demonized or "thugged out" if he throws a punch. He's ejected, suspended, and all over Sports Center for a month. That's just a punch alone, let's not even talk about a fight or a brawl a la NHL. There's a culture of fighting in the NHL, and it's okay. The media and the fans don't demonize these players like an NBA player would be, and that truly disgusts me.

I heard one dude say a while back, "Too many tattoos in the NBA." Wow. So what does that same person have to say about fighting in hockey then? Tattoos alone are too much for him, tattoos that are not hurting anyone, but what about the violence of fighting in hockey?

It's not even imaginable to have NBA brawls like NHL brawls, picture that. Ever watch some of these NHL refs break up a fight, they wait till the fighters get it in a little bit and then break it up. What a joke. Why aren't the rules and punishments for fighting tougher in hockey? Apparently, they're not!

There's a culture of fighting that they love in hockey. In the NBA, the rules and punishment are very severe, as they are in the NFL, and that's a contact sport like hockey. There are no excuses. In hockey, if you throw a punch, two minutes on the bench, in the NBA two games, not to mention how you'll be demonized. What a double standard. Unbelievable to me.

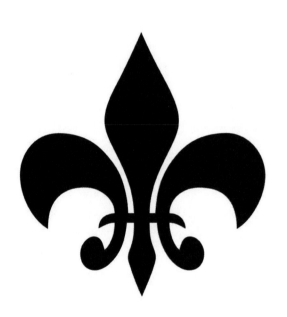

SPORTS

4. MAGIC, BIRD, DIRK, AND SEGREGATION

I once watched an NBA pre-game segment that had Magic and others as hosts. Magic did a piece on Dirk Nowitzki. On the screen was a line in the middle with Dirk on one side and the Legendary Larry Bird on the other.

Magic went on to make all these comparisons of Dirk and Bird and how alike they were. All the way to the hair and how it flowed back when they were driving to the hoop.

I love Magic. He's one of my heroes. But I thought it was disgusting and segregated.

At the time Dirk was unbelievably good, you could've compared him to anyone in the league, like Karl Malone, Darryl Dawkins, or any other great black power forward. Why just Larry Bird? Why was Steve Nash always compared to Pistol Pete? Even though they did have a similar style of circus passes, I would love the comparisons to be based on play, style, positions and not race. That's segregation of the mind, black with the black and white with the white. There's no more apartheid in life, but in sports, politics, even in high schools, yes—blacks with blacks, whites with whites, Hispanics with Hispanics. That is self-inflicted and self-made segregation.

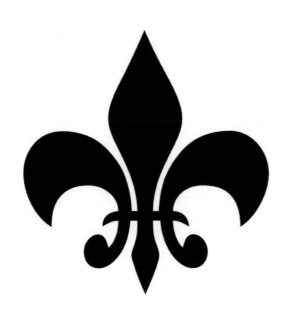

SPORTS

5. HALFTIME AT THE SUPER BOWL

Halftime at the Super Bowl is longer than the regular season or the playoffs. Way longer.

A lot of money is made during halftime at the Super Bowl. Many ads and a lot of entertainment.

My opinion on that? Bull crap, you're altering the game! A longer half means more time for a certain starter who was a little banged up to recuperate and start again at the beginning of the third quarter. How the hell do you change a game come the championship? The first game of the season should be absolutely the same as the Super Bowl—rules and time. It's a contact sport. Survival of the fittest. Why give players in the Super Bowl more time to recover for the third quarter and not in the regular season or the playoffs? For money?

I love the ads, love them, but you can't alter the game for money. The integrity of the game is lost when you take money to tweak the game a little. It's ridiculous. Why not just take an hour halftime and eat, drink, and take in all the ads as possible and all the entertainment possible and start the third quarter an hour later? Absolutely wrong for the integrity of the game. Every single game should be the same from September to February, no exceptions. Football is a game of inches and also injuries, no one should be given an extra five, ten, or fifteen minutes to regroup, but that's exactly what happens.

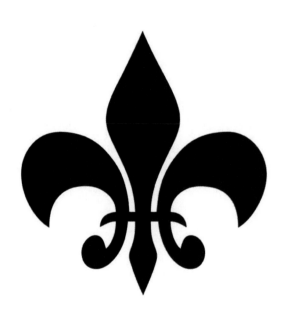

SPORTS

6. TIMEOUTS IN BASKETBALL AND FOOTBALL

In basketball you can call time basically whenever you're in trouble. Football too.

In sports there is supposed to be competition. Two teams or opponents going at it. There is a certain flow that is supposed to be uninterrupted.

My opinion on that? Damn right uninterrupted! In boxing, you get time-outs after every round. No boxer stops the fight for a time-out, unthinkable. In soccer, you play forty-five minutes a half with the game stopping only for serious injuries, and not when a certain team is in trouble and calls a time out, unthinkable. In football if there's two minutes left in the game and you are down a field goal or touchdown, and you're at your own twenty, you can methodically work your way up the field by stopping the game, time outs? Really, that's ridiculous! You're supposed to be methodical enough to know how to stop the clock; spiking the ball, running out of bounds, or just scoring on one play—that's right they're professionals. You should not stop the game with a time out, it's unfair to the other team. In soccer, a team could be down three zip with twenty minutes to go, there's no time out taking. Are you kidding me? You're supposed to be fast, methodical, and resourceful on trying to tie or win, by playing, not deliberately stopping the clock with time outs. It's silly. It's like a little kid at the playground stopping the game when he's losing.

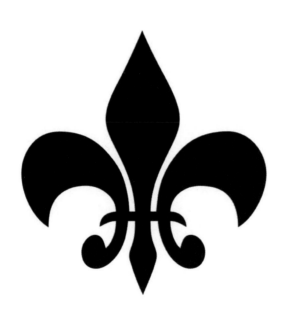

SPORTS

7. BASEBALL, GOLF, AND RACING: ARE THEY SPORTS?

Are baseball, golf, and racing a sport? Some people will take serious offense to this question. They will take offense that I made it a topic. Hey, my opinion.

We've debated this a lot in the workplace, barbershop, and bars—I know I have, a lot!

My opinion or my answer on that? Well, let's see, in baseball you can go out on defense and for three or four straight innings just stand there in right field and not do a damn thing, and get seriously paid. In football every player on defense moves, has an assignment, has a player to check, for the entire game. Same thing on offense; in baseball if you go three and out, that means you don't go bat until your turn is up the following time your team is on offense, meaning you can skip innings on offense. In football every player on offense moves, has an assignment, something to do. Basketball, too. All five players play, move, and have an assignment on offense, on defense. In tennis as well. Offense or defense, the players play.

As for golf, I truly see Tiger as an athlete, simply because he works out. Is golf a sport to me? No. A game, yes, but not a sport. I don't see Arnold Palmer as an athlete. I see JJ Watt as an athlete. I see Serena Williams as an athlete. I see Lebron James as an athlete. Arnold Palmer? No, not by a long shot. I heard a white comedian once say just because he can zoom around the corner in his mom's Buick and get gas super quick and come back, that doesn't make him an athlete. I could not agree more. I mentioned white comedian because I have a lot of white friends that agree.

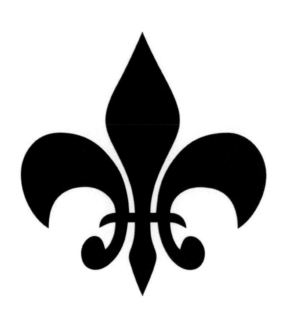

SPORTS

8. HIGH SCHOOL BALLERS

High school basketball players can't see the NBA until they're twenty years old!
This rule went into effect under David Stern citing concern for their education and injuries if they ever got hurt in their first year. Also, a factor was the big lifestyle they would be coming into at only seventeen or eighteen years of age.

My opinion on that? Bull crap! It's a discrimination of age for employment, period. Says who if I had a son and he was seventeen or eighteen that once in the NBA he wouldn't be able to handle that "lifestyle"? You don't know how I have raised my son. Also, people would say, "Oh, go to college first. Get your education and then go pro." Pfff. Okay in college are they not going to play ball? What's stopping them from breaking an ankle in college? Because they will not be playing ping-pong in college but playing basketball.

I'd rather go pro, break my ankle in my second year and continue college with a year and a half salary from the NBA that would help me tremendously in life than break an ankle in my second year in college. And who is to say you still can't go to college after going pro? That's because every black kid trying to go pro out of high school is stereotyped. Also true is that a lot of them are poor and want to help their families, so if he is truly a phenomenal player and needs the money why not go pro?

Some people go to college to become doctors; some people want to become basketball players. What is wrong with trying to go do what you want to become anyway? Kobe Bryant made the Denver hotel room mistake well into his playing days in the NBA, not his rookie year. If a player is going to be an A-hole in the league, it's because of who he is not that he came in the league straight out of high school.

The NBA should have an exemption rule like in golf. If a woman is so good, she can play with the men. Every high school baller with crazy nice talent should be able to apply for an exemption and if approved, should leap into the NBA. In hockey, baseball, gymnastics, or even racing nobody bickers when a very talented kid wants to go pro, only the NBA, only when a kid who is very poor and wants to help his family out do people bicker because he is seventeen or eighteen with no degree but on his way to millions and superstardom.

Stop the discrimination please, NBA. The NBA is employment like any other job and should stop this racist policy. If a kid has to go to college before the NBA it should be for four years, not one or two because he still has no degree. Lebron came out of high school, and Melo did one year at Syracuse. If both went to Xerox for a certain job that required a degree, they both wouldn't get the job. So what's a year or two? If you have the talent, you should apply for an exemption. Lebron could've played in the NBA at fifteen or sixteen. If I were commissioner, I would've let him.

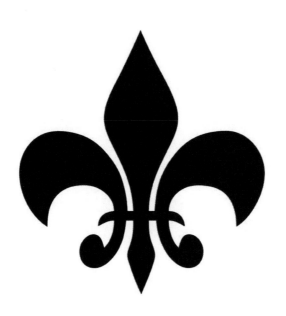

SPORTS

9. OFF-THE-FIELD ISSUES IN THE NFL

I do not condone any such behavior of violence, domestic abuse, or anything police-related by NFL players. There was a period where there was a lot of it. As commissioner, I would've been tougher than Roger Goodell. Players have kids who look up to them whether they like it or not.

My opinion on that? You got about 1,700 NFL players, and you get a stretch of fifteen to twenty-two players who happen to "cut up," meaning get arrested for all this stuff we just mentioned and the league all of sudden has an image issue? Really? Twenty-five players out of 1,700 impacting an image? No, the image is affected because of another reason. You got to be kidding. Twenty-five out of 1,700? What about the other 1,675 doing so much good in their communities with kids' football camps, charity work, church work, and high school appearances? A lot, and I mean a lot, of NFL players go out and do a lot of motivational speaking, donate on Thanksgiving, and other stuff I don't know about. But as a world, we don't care about positivity. No, we don't. We care about hearing Plaxico Burress shot himself in the leg. Yup. Negativity always dominates positivity. People don't care about the annual Rolland Williams football camp at East High School in Rochester, people care about Adrian Peterson whooping his kid with a tree branch, a switch, or a stick. Twenty-five out of 1,700? Give me a break.

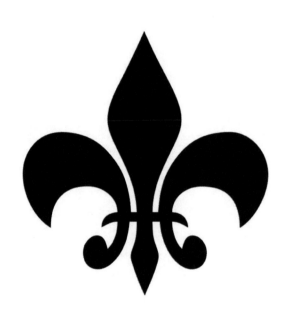

SPORTS

10. The greatness of MJ

Michael Jordan: argued by many and most as the best ever. Outstanding numbers.

All kinds of hardware to prove it.

My opinion on that? Yes, without a single doubt. Michael built championships where he was, in Chicago. He didn't take his talents to South Beach to look for a championship. Dwayne Wade was already Dwayne Wade, with a championship, when he was joined by Lebron. Shaq was already Shaq, the most dominating force in the league, when they hooked with Kobe. Scottie Pippen was a baby in Chicago and learned, developed, and blossomed under Michael. Michael won three championships back-to-back, took a couple of years off, came back, and did it again. That is something no one ever did and will never do again. Two years off? And then you do it again? Not one or two, but three in a row?

I want to see Lebron, Kobe, or Kevin Durant, or anyone do that. If Magic and Bird couldn't, no one will. Hakeem Olajuwon can thank Michael for the rest of his life for his rings, because Michael could've won eight in a row, the Rockets won two back-to-back in MJ's absence. I don't even want to get into the statistics. But the ones I love, back to back forty-plus point games with the Wizards, at forty years of age. Wow. Did Shaq, Magic, Bird, Hakeem, Charles, David (Robinson), Isaiah, Kareem, Dominque play at that age? And have back-to-back forty-plus point games? Will Kobe? Lebron? Dwayne? That's talent and durability.

Jeff van Gundy, I like you today. But once I thought you were the biggest idiot on the planet. Trying to go at Michael because Michael would be professional, nice, and joking with his opponents before games and then get on the court and be an absolute assassin—shredding and ripping them apart. That's exactly what you're supposed to do. Good sportsmanship is being nice before and after games. What did you want Michael to do, score only twenty and not sixty-three? Miss layups? Not dunk on people? Not torch people? Not play defense? Smile and joke around on the court? No, he didn't get paid for that. He got paid to torch his opponent as hard as possible, to win games. Did you want him to be new generation? Rude? Arrogant? Never shake hands before or after games? One who hated his opponents on and off the court? You were an idiot for saying what you said, but I like you today. You're very basketball-savvy and one of the best analysts and commentators today.

RACE

1. DEFINITION OF RACISM

There's a definition for racism in the dictionary.

The general feeling or thought of racism or the word racism is white people hating or discriminating minorities.

Racism is a serious cancer in the world, and it will always be around.

My opinion on that? I don't know what the dictionary says about racism. To me, racism is simply making race an issue when you're not supposed to, simple as that. However, my definition of racist is someone who does not like a certain or certain races, and someone who makes race an issue on a daily basis in his or her everyday life, simple as that. Can we cut the crap please? I know a lot of black folks and Latinos who are racists, the general thought of just whites being racist is silly. Why is it that when a black, Latino, Arab, Asian or Arab mimics a white person it's okay, but when a white person mimics a black, Latino, Arab, or Asian person it's racist? Bull crap! For like five years straight, inner city kids, all blacks and Latino, in my city, had these fights and brawls arranged on the internet. They would have them at the family amusement park or the beach with families around. Some of us denounced this very strongly, on the news and on the radio. It was okay for us to do that, we were "responsible citizens." Not the white folks, though. If you're white and denounce all this barbaric foolishness of these inner-city kids who were all black and Latino, you're a racist, pfff!

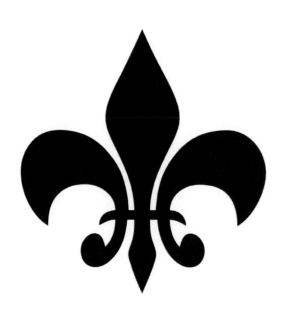

RACE

2. BIRACIALNESS

Some people are against interracial couples.
They say interracial couples only hurt the kids they have with the teasing, bullying, and pressures at school.

They are completely against biracialness (my own word).

My opinion on that? Barack Obama, Bob Marley, Derek Jeter, Jason Kidd, Tiger Woods, Colin Powell, Halle Berry, Alicia Keys, Mariah Carey, Jordin Sparks, Yannick Noah, and so many more, should not be around. Everything Bob Marley did and the music he left us shouldn't be. Everything Tiger did in golf should not had happened. Everything DJ (Derek Jeter) did in the Bronx should not have happened. I should not have my Mariah Carey catalogue at all. Give me a break. As for the teasing and the bullying and the pressures—educate your own kids properly not to make fun of people. What's truly silly is there's nothing to make fun of here. Nothing but the people who make fun of people. It's just pure ignorance, stupidity, and just being dumb. It boggles my mind how people like to call the shots on who you should be with, you yourself don't even call those shots—it's your heart. I might have a preference of let's say a beautiful cocoa-skinned black woman, yet at work my heart might just fall for this gorgeous Hispanic chick, or Caucasian, or Arab, or Asian.

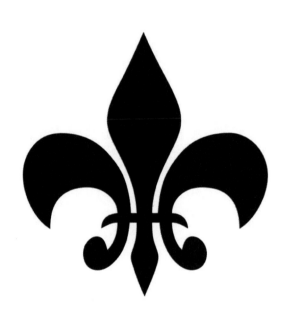

RACE

3. *The dumbest thing I ever heard ever*

I've heard it. You may have heard it, too.

You hear it a lot in the hood. You will hear it amongst very ignorant and dumb people, of any race. You will hear, "Oh, you tryna be white?"

My opinion on that? Going to school to further your education, get a good job, and raise a family is not "tryna be white". In the past, that's what I've heard a lot of people say. In my experience, in the black community, especially in the inner-city, when you opt to leave the "game" (stop selling drugs) and go to school, it's "tryna be white." When you spoke properly, in the hood, you're "tryna be white." If you go to the library and try to just go and relax and read, nothing more, then you're trying to be white. If you try to dress properly, button-up tucked in some kakis with a nice pair of loafers, you're trying to be white. Absolutely disgusting and ignorant. But the most absurd one is the school one—that's just the dumbest thing ever. When a young person in the hood tries to talk properly and go to school to turn his life around from previous mistakes or bad choices, he's trying to be white. Lord God, please help us!

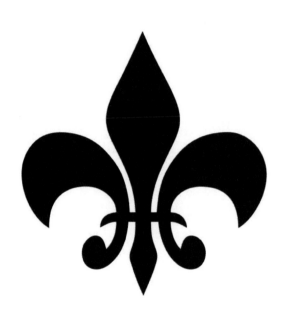

RACE

4. INNER-CITY KIDS AND FARM KIDS

In my city, there's been a lot of violence with the inner-city youth. Violence at home (neighborhoods), violence at school, and violence in public.

I'm talking middle and high school kids.

A lot of parents, a lot of people in general, usually would call into radio shows and blame the schools, blame the teachers, blame the city. They would blame the whole world.

They would say the city needs to provide better activities for them to do after school.

My opinion on that? Cut the crap! There's plenty, plenty, plenty to do in the city. Farm kids sometimes are bored out of their minds but they're not going to kill each other. Take a good look at what the inner city has to offer, in terms of recreation and other activities compared to these suburban farm kids. If you have to compare, the farm kids have zero to do, zero. Raise your kids right. From the time they come into this world, grab their little hand and start the teaching. Do not wait on the teachers, city officials, or some new Boys and Girls Club to do your job for you. All those other things I just mentioned are fine and dandy but they're not you. Your child comes home to you and answers to you, not the teachers or the city officials. All the violence in neighborhoods, schools and in public by these kids is their own fault, them, their parents or households. Raise your kids right, from the jump, teach them how to talk properly and be involved with them every day showing them what's right and what's wrong.

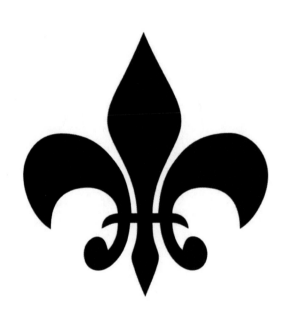

RACE

5. A CRAZY STORY

When I was like twelve years old, I experienced a bizarre yet horrible incident that I will never forget. It happened in Albany, New York, my childhood city. My sister, parents, and I were visiting some friends of the family in a nice middle-class neighborhood. We were visiting overnight (the weekend). I had brought my bike along so I wouldn't get too bored. So one of the two days, I went on my little bike ride through this very nice neighborhood and—bam—the craziest and most bizarre thing ever happened. While riding on the sidewalk of a certain block, a little kid about six years old stands in his doorway with the door open and says to me, "Hey, you, our sidewalk wasn't made for black people to ride on." I stopped and said, "What did you say?" Then a man in his late forties came to the door behind the kid and asked what was going on. I said to him, "Ask him what he just said to me." After telling the man what the little boy said, the man surprisingly started whooping the little boy and asking him why he said that.

You would think he got that from the man whom I believed was his father but nope, from what I saw and how I remember that man, that little boy did not get that from that man. I got back on my bike and continued my ride and at the time wasn't too shocked, but looking back it's very shocking and very sad.

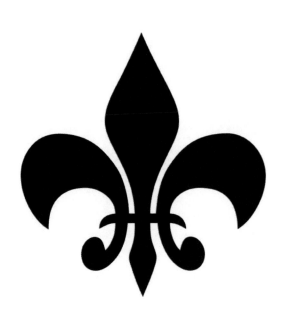

RACE

6. WAY TOO MANY BLACK ASSOCIATIONS

Definition of association: an alliance of people for a certain cause. That's my definition. I didn't even bother looking it up.

Black folks have a lot of these. Association of black this, association of black that.

There are so many today.

My opinion on that? Ridiculous. Yes, it's ridiculous. If it has something to do with black history, yes, I'm all for it and support it 100%. If not, then it's segregation. I feel they should be illegal. They're racist and unnecessary and make race an issue when they're not supposed to. If I go uptown and get a great bagel baked by a black baker and then tomorrow go to Brooklyn and get another great bagel baked by another black baker, guess what's gonna happen? That's right, the association of black bakers is what you're going to get. Black lawyers, black scholars, black this, black that—it's wrong. We love to divide and segregate with this black thing. Can we not just join the world and excel at whatever we do without these groups and associations? Same for Latinos, Arabs, or Asians—if you're good or have a lot of people of your race in a certain field, stop these groups and associations. It keeps us divided. None of these associations' arguments are valid to me unless it has something to do with the history of the race. If not, it is racist and segregative.

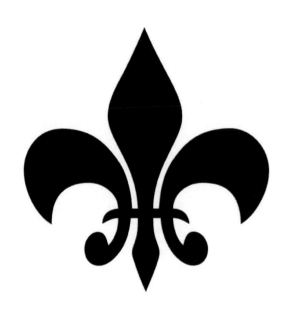

RACE

7. *A WHITE GUY TRYING TO BE BLACK*

I used to hear this a lot in the work place, barbershops, basketball games.

When a white guy loves black girls, black style of clothes, black music, he's trying to be black. Especially if all he wears are Nike Air Force Ones.

My opinion on that? Get over it. The man simply likes or loves black, end of story. One has to not like his or her own race simply because he or she loves black culture? It's ridiculous! I had a supervisor who knew more about hip-hop than so many of my black friends I have and listened with in the past. I had another supervisor who, along with the other supervisor, knew just as much about Wu-Tang as me and more than anyone else I knew.

Both of them are white and married to white women, get over it. Jon B, fabulous R&B singer, who's Jewish, has never tried to be black nor has Robin Thicke. They simply love black, but are not trying to be black. My favorite actors and actresses are all white except for Morgan Freeman, Denzel Washington, and Angela Bassett. I drink tea. I've been wearing Levi's when my black friends thought they were corny and too white. I listen to classical music (R&B, Hip-hop, Reggae, and Rumba too). I watch all of the Winter Olympics. Am I trying to be white here? In the hood most would say yes. Give me a break. They happen to be things and people that I like and love. End of story. I don't give a damn what a person thinks of what I love. That's their ignorance.

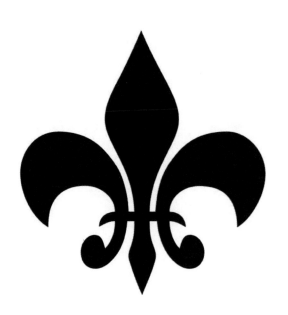

RACE

8. BRINGING HOME A BLACK MAN

To some, it's a non-issue except to the ignorant.

It goes both ways—bringing home a white dude or a Hispanic is supposed to be a non-issue. Unfortunately, it's not.

My opinion on that? A friend of mine once told me that a friend of his, a white chick, told him, "You don't know many of us white girls love black men and would like to be with them but are afraid of what our families would say."

Another time I listened to someone older tell a younger person, both black, to never bring home a white man. I sat there not believing what I just heard.

So sad and ridiculous. Shame on all of you who pressure your loved ones into this racist mentality. I've dated all races. I used to be scared to marry another race for fear that even though my girl might love me, it didn't mean her family would, thus problems. Then I snapped out of that. I decided if ever I loved someone who loved me, and both of us wanted to be together forever despite the ignorance of family, then so be it.

When shopping, we buy what we like and love, period. No one dictates what is good or bad for your wardrobe. You choose your colors and sizes. Your taste matters over anybody's.

Same for love—love who you love, period. Follow your heart, it always tells the truth. You can never go wrong when you follow your heart, your choice will always be genuine.

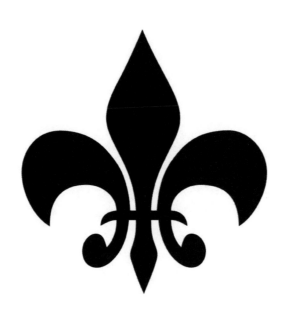

RACE

9. NO WHITE PRIDE

It's okay to shout black pride or black is beautiful.

It's also okay to shout or have Latino pride.

When you shout white pride, you're a racist.

My opinion on that? No race on this planet is despised like the black race. No race has been made fun of and been mistreated like the black race. Four hundred years is a very long time. When a race screams or says the word pride like the black race, it's not a joke, or a game. We have pride of being around today and standing proud of where we came from, what we went through, and what we've been called. It's not a joke. No race went through four hundred years of what the black race went through. No race throughout the world goes through what the black race goes through. Every race experiences racism and mistreatment. Not like the black race. No race is made fun of like the black race, no name-calling like the black race, throughout history. All races get their share, just not like the black race. We experience racism and discrimination like no other race.

Reason we say we have black pride. Proud of having everything we have physically that the world makes fun of. From our skin to our noses and everything else that's been said throughout history. We're proud that the slave of yesterday went from chains to being called Denzel Washington, Oprah Winfrey, Steve Harvey, Angela Bassett, Michael Jordan, Serena Williams, and Nasir Jones.

It is not to say you can't have white pride, Latino pride, Asian or Arab. Everyone should be proud of their race, it's not even an issue. I love Black History Month. It is crucial that the youth know where they came from because black history is a gigantic part of American history.

As a young black student, black history should be such an inspiring subject, a subject to propel you to the stars. No White pride? Of course, there should be pride in all races, period. The title of this segment isn't literal in anyway at all. I trust I have some intelligent readers—it's sarcastic.

RACE

10. THE GAY LABEL

Anything we don't understand we fear.

Most of the time we label it weird or gay. It's so common among the general populace to just call something or someone gay because they're unusual.

It's super ignorant and the second dumbest thing ever.

My opinion on that? I just said it, super ignorant. I used to joke with my co-workers at my night job, that when any of them liked a particular country song it was okay—they're all white. But if I, a black man, like a particular country song, I'm gay to some people. Yes, there's that kind of ignorance out there, especially in the inner-city.

Another thing was fashion. I used to talk to them about this, too. I wore $125 cologne, nice European clothes you don't see every day, and $600, $800, and $1200 shoes, but no one had seen my girlfriend yet so to some I was gay. Can you believe that? Unbelievable! So if a black man wears $500 sandals and you haven't seen his girl yet, he's gay? Whatever!

And to the so-called thugs who back in the day loved the baggy jeans and baggy clothing and used to call us gay for wearing slim-fit jeans, what are you guys wearing today? The so-called thugs are wearing super tight jeans and sagging them. If we were gay for wearing slim-fit jeans back in the day, the so-called thugs have to be super gay then, because my jeans were never that tight. Stop the ignorance please. If you don't like or understand one's fashion, it doesn't make him or her gay.

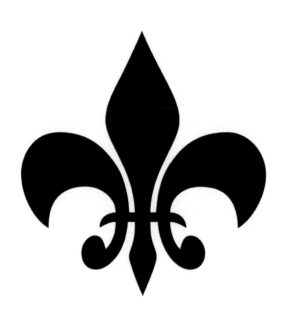

RELIGION

1. THE POPULATION OF THE EARTH

I'm a firm believer in the Lord Jesus Christ. I believe the Bible as the word of God. I believe in church.
 I had to put that on the table as we talk about faith, religion, and beliefs.

There's a question I've had since childhood: after God made Adam and Eve, they had children. So how did we populate?

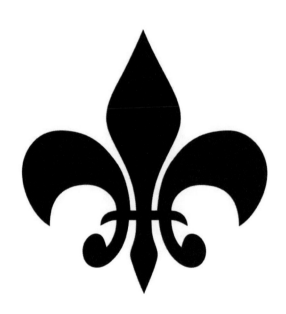

RELIGION

2. MIRACLES

There are miracles that happen every day in our lives.

All kinds of miracles from God.

There's also a "Super-Miracle," that's what I call it.

Super-Miracles are what I read about in the Bible—Jesus walking on water, the blind being able to see, and the crippled standing up and walking after being prayed on.

My opinion on that? Not saying it doesn't happen anymore or that it's impossible, but my entire life that I have lived, I have never ever one time seen with my own eyes or heard of anyone who was completely blind, pitch-black vision from birth, be prayed on and be able to see. I have never seen a crippled person from birth, in a wheelchair, go to the podium, be prayed on and stand up and walk. I have never seen a deaf and dumb person be prayed on and be instantly delivered, ever. Never saw it or heard it in my circle of people who witnessed it first-hand.

I saw an Evangelist on TV one Sunday morning pray over a deaf and dumb person and claim the person was delivered and healed by Jesus to the crowd. Even when this person was clearly still the same as he was when his family brought him on stage, as they were walking off the stage the person was still the same, but the Evangelist was jumping for joy and pumping up the crowd and saying, "Look at the miracle Jesus just performed. He's delivered."

Really? The Super Miracles do happen, I just never in my life witnessed one.

RELIGION

3. CELEBRATING CHRISTIAN HOLIDAYS

There are two major Christian holidays we celebrate a year: Easter and Christmas. These holidays pertain to Jesus Christ.

In America, we have come to twist these holidays completely around.

My opinion on that? The Easter bunny has no place in Easter. Santa Claus has no place in Christmas. If you don't believe in God or if you don't believe in Jesus Christ as Lord and Savior, then stay away from his holidays and make your own. These two holidays are completely business and entertainment today, instead of faith and remembrance. So many parents talk about raising their kids right. Well do that. Start by explaining truly what Easter is and what Christmas is, and don't bring up any bunnies or fat dudes in a red suit. You got some people who don't even believe in God but yet are exchanging gifts at Christmas, huh? They don't believe in Islam neither and would never go to a mosque or partake in any Muslim activities. So if you don't believe in God or Jesus Christ as Lord and Savior, why do you do anything on Christmas? Your wife and your kids too, why do you do anything on Christmas? It's not Santa's day, it's the Lord's day. Stop being fake and be real, even if you have to be in a corner by yourself while the rest of us celebrate Jesus, but do not destroy Easter and Christmas by replacing it with a bunch of crap because you don't believe in God and Jesus.

RELIGION

4. Christian Churches in the Middle East today

Christians have churches. Muslims have mosques.

These two religions are practiced all over the world. They are the two dominating faiths in the world. They are based on the Lord Jesus Christ for Christianity and the Prophet Muhammad for Islam.

One should be free to believe in and congregate with whomever he chooses among the two faiths.

My opinion on that? I have a big problem with how Muslims are free to build mosques all over the world how they want, but I cannot go to the Middle East and build a church and practice my Christianity. I have no problems whatsoever with Islam, Arabs, or the Prophet Muhammad, that's all irrelevant right here. I'm talking about how up and down and across America there are mosques everywhere and people are free to practice their Islamic faith. Try that in the Middle East, you can't go there and build churches how you want and practice Christianity how you want. It's unfair. I have a huge problem with that. No one is killing Muslims in the States because they're Muslim, but they do that sometimes to Christians in the Middle East. Not fair. You are free to do what you want in my house, but not in your house? Not fair. I'm not saying close down the mosques in America, no, but let people build churches in the Middle East and practice their faith as Muslims do around the world, very simple.

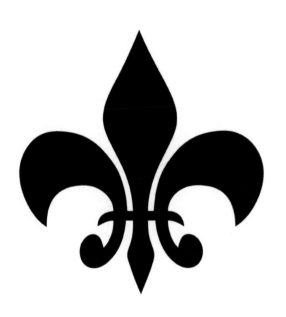

RELIGION

5. ISLAM AND TERRORISM

People love to associate terrorism with Islam.

Since 9/11 terrorism has become the number one topic or issue in the world today.

Terrorists who are Muslim are called Islamic terrorists or Islamic extremists.

My opinion on that? Bull crap! Islam and terrorism are not associated. These people who bomb and kill are not Islamic terrorists or Islamic extremists, they are simply terrorists, they are simply extremists, who use the name Islam to justify their evil. Nowhere in the Koran will you find a justification for what they do. Islam is a faith of tranquility and peace. I'm a Christian and reject any notion that Islam is evil or supports terrorism and violence. I have a friend, a great dude, who is Muslim. I'd rather hang with him than with so many other "Christian" people I know who are complete jerks. I'm with President Obama. I refuse to associate Islam with anything terrorists (Muslim terrorists) do. They have their agenda and philosophy for wanting to kill, and they label it with Islam, and a lot of people around the globe have bought it. There is no God or religion that inspires, instructs or supports any of these evil acts. Timothy McVeigh was a terrorist, not an American or Christian terrorist, but simply a terrorist. Terrorists in the Middle East are simply that, too—terrorists.

My dear Parents

Our Family, saying good-bye to my Dad.

My Mom, nephew & nieces;
Rolly, Mireille & Love.

Fanny & Wendy, my Fiancee
& my beautiful daughter.

Me & Mom

The Tshisekedis, my Uncle & Aunt with my cousin Kamo, the 2011 elected
President of the Democratic Republic of Congo,
brother and a dear friend of my late Father.

The Kayemba Family, my Uncle & Aunt, here celebrating 50 years of Marriage, very special.

Monique, a very dear friend, lives in London England.

Me and Cindy, another very dear friend, last summer out celebrating my birthday.

Co-workers(bosses and a good friend, Matt)clockwise; Rick, me, Matt & Mike.

The absolute best, Mike Palumbo, my boss.

RELIGION

6. *Women's rights in the Middle East today*

Women don't have the same rights as men in some or all countries in the Middle East.

Women don't enjoy everyday liberties, like driving, that women do in America.

Women are prohibited by some extremists in certain regions from going to school, from getting an education.

My opinion on that? Okay, let's say we, the rest of the world, say, "You guys are right, we're gonna follow you." Say we said that 2,000 years ago, what would the world look like today? The whole globe, no female drivers, and for the extremists who prohibit young girls from getting an education, imagine that...no female students or scholars....really? Imagine the world today according to these extremists. I'm with President Obama and so many more people—equal pay, equal rights, equal opportunities for women around the globe. A man can be the head of the household but that does not mean that he owns his wife, that she's an object. A woman in the Middle East should be able to drive her husband to the hospital if he's sick or drive to the mall if she wants to. She should be able to go to school and find a cure for cancer. Science and technology can go forward with men and women. Why cut your chances of improving the world in half? Women are the other half.

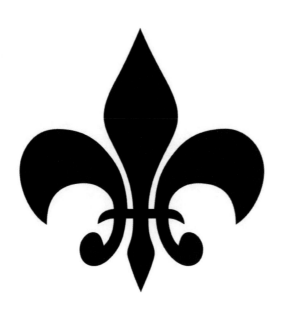

RELIGION

7. *FAITH AND RELIGION*

We all know what religion is.
  We all know what faith is.

They're very distinct. Religion is more physical to me, but faith is of the heart, the mind, what you truly believe. Religion is more of a routine than a belief.

My opinion on that? Just that, religion is a routine, a label. It will not get you in Heaven. How your heart is will. Sure there are practices that come with each faith, and I'd rather talk about Christianity here because that's all I know and all I believe in. Yes, you have to believe (faith). Yes, you have to go to church. Yes, you have to be baptized. Yes, you have to tithe. Yes, you have to give offerings, help out at the church, and go pick up church members with the church van if you can. All that is good. With a bad heart and no faith and no love for others, all of that good stuff becomes religion. It all becomes empty. Nothing but routine. Like an NFL player or soccer player going on the field and making a sign of the cross is just a routine. True faith has nothing to do with the physical or a routine or how much you tithe or donate. It's all about your heart, what you believe in. There has to be belief and love behind everything you do, and you have to know, understand, and love what you do (practices and activities), or it's just religion. Religion can be a bad word to me and it can also be a good word, when everything you do is backed by faith and love. Amen to that!

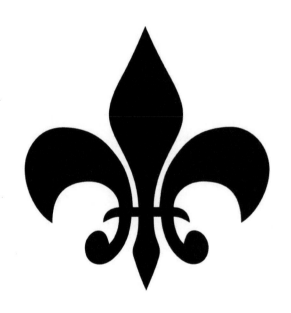

RELIGION

8. THE SPINNING OF THE EARTH

The Earth turns, spins, and moves.

Scientists have a perfect explanation for the spinning of the earth.

I love science. I love technology. I love gadgets.

My opinion on this? I respect scientists. I don't respect any scientist who rejects God. I don't think for one second, that inside the Earth, dead in the middle is a huge mechanical device that makes the world go around. Neither do you. Give me all the explanations on why or how the Earth spins and I won't believe you. God makes it spin. God makes it turn. Every day. No question about it.

The same way I believe he created the Universe, the planets, the planet Earth, and all it has—man and animals. I don't believe in evolution. Only God could create such things in uniform. We all have arms with hands with ten fingers, legs, and feet with ten toes. How can evolution have such a uniform way of evolving? How come monkeys have stopped evolving into humans? What happened?

People and scientists love to believe that we're not alone, that there's life or was life on Mars. If there is and there was, God put it there. I don't see the air in my lungs, but without a single doubt it's there and I know this. I don't see God and his angels physically, but I know they're around me, all the time, without a single doubt.

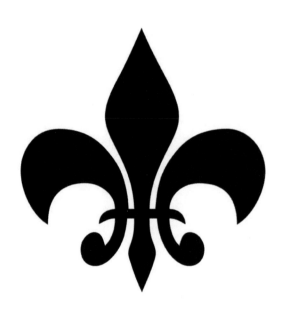

RELIGION

9. THE WORLD AND THE CHURCH

I once heard or was preached to about the world and the church, the church and the world.

An evangelist once made a fascinating analysis of the two.

It stuck with me forever.

He said he once looked for the world and he found it in the church, and he also looked for the church and he found it in the world. Fascinating. So true.

He meant that if you go in the church today, you'll find the world—people full of hypocrisy, jealousy, gossip, arrogance, lies, lust, adultery, and fornication (yup that's you). You can go into the world today and find the church. People who don't even believe in God, yet the most beautiful people ever; very kind, hospitable, always donating to the poor and needy, faithfully married, full of love, compassion, respect, generosity and humanity.

Just because a person goes to church means zero to me, and just because a person doesn't go to church still means zero to me, in terms of their character. It's who you are in life, not where you go physically. A good friend once told me, "It's not who you are deep down inside, but what you do that defines who you are." It's so true—all that deep down inside crap is just a load of crap and excuses. Going to church is great, but it's not, as a Christian, the key to going to Heaven or being a good person. Being a good person is simply that, being a good person.

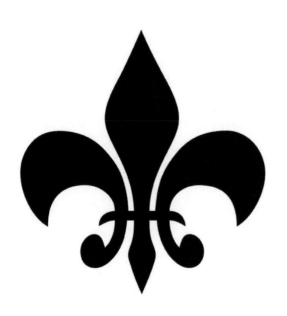

RELIGION

10. CONFESSING MY FAITH

My faith is simple, and always will be. I believe in God. I believe in Jesus Christ as Lord and Savior. I believe God created the Universe, Earth, and everything on it. I believe the path to salvation goes through the Lord Jesus Christ. I believe in Heaven, and I believe there's a hell. If there is God, then there's a devil. I respect anyone trying and wanting to go to Heaven, whether a Christian or a Muslim. Some people believe in God and have these weird religions that have real bizarre practices. I don't judge them, especially the congregations. In their minds, they truly believe they're serving God. Some of them were brain washed from a very early age. That's all they know, is this real bizarre religion, you see. Do not judge them. There is only one God and one Heaven in my belief, and one book only that I believe as the word of God, the Holy Bible.

Whether of faith or not, religious or not, I believe in doing unto others as you would like done unto you, and not doing unto others as you would not like done unto you, it's called Karma by many. Everything you do comes back to you, good or bad, there's no ducking it. I've tried to be as generous as possible my whole life. I believe God gives you back way more than you give, always. I would love to start a ministry of giving.

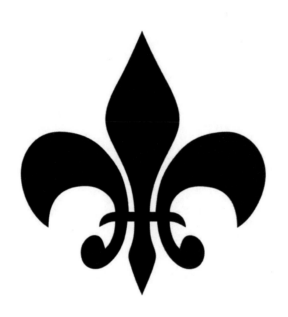

Bonus

Michael Vick's return • Peyton Manning's recovery• Serena Williams' dominance • Lame participation trophies • The gay label • Gay fashion designers • The world is pretty big • Dumb beauty pageants • Howard Stern, Michael Jordan, Clayton Kershaw • The digital age and music • Tom Cruise's no-show • Fast-food • Mark Zuckerberg's genius •Hyundai • Italy • Japan • Germany • Commercials • Polygraphs • My favorites today • 9/11 • Mayor Rudy Giuliani • The Paris attacks • Prisons and education • The rich lifestyle • Blood and love • Comedy and insults • A beautiful woman • Criticizing Valentine's Day • The other ill • The University of Notre Dame • Tickets • The tackiest things • Using the bathroom • Obesity and poverty • Gifts • We human beings • I love New York • Determination

Michael Vick's return

On November 15, 2010, Michael Vick had the best game by an NFL quarterback, the best game in NFL History. Philly vs. Washington, Landover Maryland. His numbers? Vick completed his first ten passes, finished twenty for twenty-eight for 333 yards and four touchdowns. He ran eight times for eighty yards and two touchdowns. The Eagles set team records for total yards in a game, 592. They also scored forty-five points in the first half, another team record. They led thirty-five to zip after the first quarter, a record, for since 1950, the biggest lead for a road team was 28-0. Vick became the first player in NFL history with at least 300 yards passing, and fifty yards rushing, and six touchdowns, four passing and two rushing. With no interceptions. Are you kidding me?

Let's not even talk about the moves while running. Who in NFL history had better numbers in one game? Along with the razzle dazzle? Who? No one. If this was Peyton (who is, in my opinion, the best ever) or Tom or Aaron, all phenomenal QBs, this game would've went straight to DVD and at your local Walmart and Target the next day. Oh yeah, I forgot the Eagles won 59-28.

The numbers don't begin at all to tell the story of what he did that Monday night. I watched in disbelief. Vick was amazing that night. He wasn't human, only a cape was missing. So many sports shows only talked about this game for a couple of days. Are you kidding me? Cut the crap. Would you do the same if it was Tom Brady, Peyton Manning, and Aaron Rodgers? Dog killer or not, performance is performance, period. He paid his price, his punishment. He did his time. He lost a lot of money, respect, dignity, and opportunities. He corrected himself. America is a country of dog lovers, which is great, but the man paid his price for his actions. I also know America to be a country of forgiveness and second chances. I was very happy to see a lot of people of all color do that for Michael. I salute you Mike, best game ever, best game in NFL history.

Peyton Manning's recovery

Peyton Manning, I salute you for not only being the best ever, but for what you did for your team when you came back from all those procedures (surgeries). You took your team to the big dance, the Super Bowl, unbelievable. You made it seem so easy, but I know it wasn't. Just going to the Super Bowl was enough for me—you didn't have to win it at all to prove anything to me. You were a champion already. Two years off, and you come back and go straight to the show. Wow, hats off to you. People could only talk about how and that Denver lost. What about talking about what he went through and still making it to the dance? I'm not making excuses for the loss. No, the loss is irrelevant here, got demolished fair and square (shout out to Russell Wilson).

I'm just praising Peyton for what so many people didn't and don't talk about—his comeback! Some athletes have one major procedure and they're done for their career. Enter Penny Hardaway. Penny Hardaway played for the Orlando Magic in the mid 90s. Penny was ridiculously nice, I even had his shoes. After he got hurt—bam—he was done. He never recovered. Penny's story is a travesty, one of the saddest stories in NBA history in terms of talent.

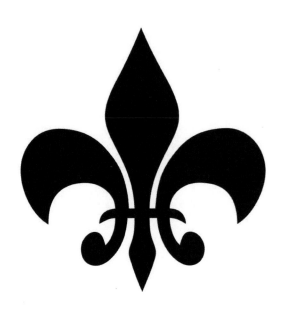

Serena Williams's dominance

Serena Williams, I salute you. Super talent you have. Super fit, super trainer, super determined, and a super ferocious winning attitude on the court (no smiling).

Twenty-one Grand Slam titles, including four in a row, calendar year or not, doesn't matter, does not. People cannot really grasp this, placing all four trophies on your living room table at home, and saying to yourself, "I won four majors in a row. I beat the best of the best, on all surfaces, in all four Grand Slams." Wow. We love you, Serena. Dominance.

Lame participation trophies

Participation trophies? Really? Yeah, right. We're turning our kids into a nation of losers. Participating is not winning. You make them lazy with these lame trophies. They won't work hard to become real champions because they know they'll be getting a trophy anyway, a lame one.

The gay label

If you're black, dress nice, smell nice, wear $500 Italian shoes, and no one has seen your girlfriend yet, you're gay. Yup, that's what they're saying behind your back. Trust me, I've been there. The gay label— what ignorance.

Gay fashion designers

Speaking of gay, why are all the great fashion designers gay? (Ralph is straight.) Versace, McQueen, Ford, dead and alive, genius designers (male) are all gay. I'm not saying it's a crime. I'm saying why can't a lot of straight men be geniuses at designing men and women clothing? It's taboo or funny for a man to sit down and draw nice clothing for women? It's perplexing to me.

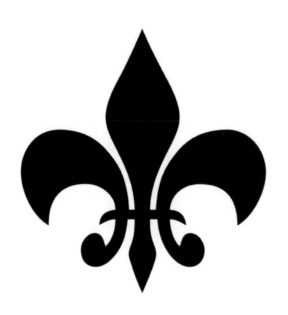

The world is pretty big

The world has gotten a lot smaller with the latest innovations of the tech world, Internet, and Facebook. However, it took a year and change for us to find out what happened to Malaysia flight MH17. What's really mind-boggling is, we couldn't even find it. I mean, the world is pretty big after all—the sea is bigger and deeper than I thought. With all the tech gurus and aviation experts, we couldn't even find this aircraft or pieces of it. Bits and pieces had to surface before any sighting or finding. The world is pretty big.

Dumb beauty pageants

Isn't it just sad how dumb some beauty pageants can be? I mean it is super sad. Is beauty the only thing they know? Some of them are just dumb as a rock. Unbelievable!

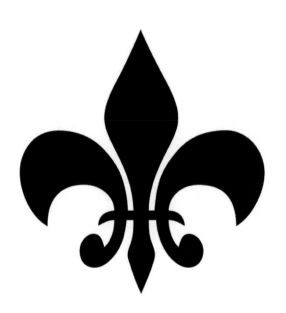

Howard Stern, Michael Jordan, and Clayton Kershaw

Howard Stern, Michael Jordan, and Clayton Kershaw—unbelievable numbers. Dollars that is. They started it, and I love it. Howard Stern started off with a $500 million contract. Michael Jordan made thirty million plus a year in his last two seasons as a Bull—still not enough to compensate him for all of the years he went so underpaid in Chicago. Michael should've made thirty million a year his whole career because he made money for everyone. When he and the Bulls came to town everybody made money—the NBA, TV ratings, the other team, the arenas, the merchandise, the city, everybody. Clayton Kershaw? Three hundred million dollars for ten years ($30M a year)—why get mad at me? Get mad at the owner, the team, and the people in the room who said yes. End of story.

As a player, a good one, I am obligated to ask for as much as I can, if they say no, fine, if they say yes even better. Get mad at who said yes and not me. If a person making ten dollars an hour asked for ten more—twenty dollars an hour—and they gave it to him or her, would he or she turn it down?

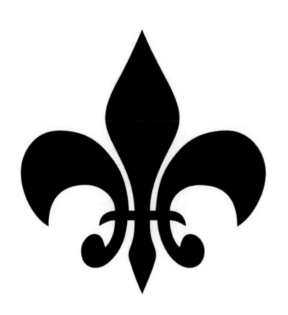

The digital age and music

One hundred thousand copies for Janet Jackson's "Unbreakable" sold in its first week. Are you kidding me? This is Janet Jackson we're talking here—100,000 copies? Technology, the digital era is a gift and a curse. It used to be 300,000 or 400,000 easy if your name was Janet.

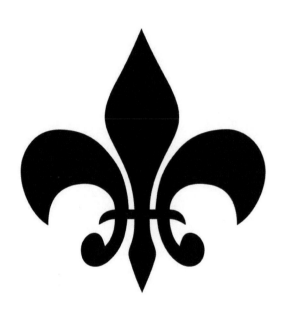

Tom Cruise's no-show

Tom Cruise was supposedly a "no-show" at his daughter's wedding. A no-show? A news program said just that. I watched it myself early in the morning before going to work. Then I thought, really? How do you people know he was a no-show? Did he say he was going to their wedding? A no-show is someone who commits to an event and doesn't show up. Was that the case? Did his daughter say that? Do you people know the Cruise family? Do you know all the details of this wedding? No. Why report on something you haven't a clue about? That's not news anymore, that's gossip.

Fast food is very expensive

Fast food? Why is it so expensive? I once spent almost eight bucks (seven and change) at a popular fast food spot and forty-five minutes later, when I got home, I was hungry again.

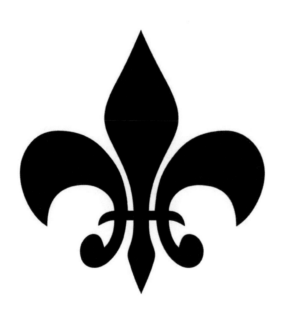

Mark Zuckerberg's genius

Mark Zuckerberg, a genius, yes. Facebook is one of the greatest inventions ever—right up there with the telephone, that's right, my opinion. Can you imagine what he would be worth if he charged just $10 or $5 a month or $1 to every Facebook user in the world? That's power. That's genius.

Hyundai

Hyundai Genesis? A luxury Hyundai? Doesn't sound right. Toyota has Lexus. Honda has Acura. Nissan has Infiniti. Hyundai should go with the program and build a separate luxury line, it sounds better. When I'm driving a Toyota, I feel like I'm driving a regular automobile, but when I'm driving a Lexus, I feel like I'm driving a luxury automobile. Big difference.

Italy

Is it just me who can't get over the beauty of Italy? Everything Italian is beautiful, everything. The cars, the clothes, the shoes. Let's not bring up shoes—I own too many pairs of Italian made shoes. The fragrances, the food, the land, landscapes, Florence, Venice (sits on water), Rome, the language, the race—yes the race has always had that mystique, mystery. Look at a picture of the Italian National Soccer Team. You would think it's Puerto Rico's or Mexico's or a country from South America. Everything Italian is simple, yet chic and beautiful.

Japan

While we're speaking of countries, everything British is classic and above everybody else (British pound). Everything Japanese is also simple, yet beautiful just like Italy. Beautiful and full of grace. When something is from and made in Japan, it's crafted with intelligent engineering only from Japan. There's something about that "MADE IN JAPAN" label. To me it means quality, durability, and no compromises.

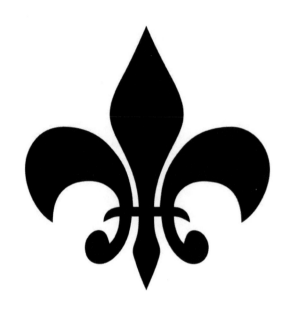

Germany

And last, but not least, is Germany. My father once told me that when he was younger he and his colleagues used to call the Japanese the Germans of the East. I can't add anything to that. He meant to praise the intelligence, engineering, and craftsmanship of the Germans. Anyone who can create an automobile like the Mercedes Benz and keep the quality, integrity, engineering, technology, and styles just going, going, and going and staying at the top forever gets all the praises in the world from me. All praises due. Did I mention Audi? And BMW?

Commercials

Commercials after Obama winning office—when does it stop? The ass kissing and patronizing of black people in commercials. Unreal. All the bad guys are always white and the good guys are always black. It's insane. The dumb guy is always white and the smart guy is always, always black. It really offends the crap out of me.

As a black person, I feel like our race is treated like the handicapped—always favored and untouchable in commercials... Pfff, it's pathetic. Since 2008, it's been unreal. Especially in the Kia commercial where the little white kid is the bad baseball player and the black kid is the good one who just won a Championship (just to get a lame participation trophy). But the point here is, even with the kids, it doesn't stop—white is bad, black is good. Cut the crap.

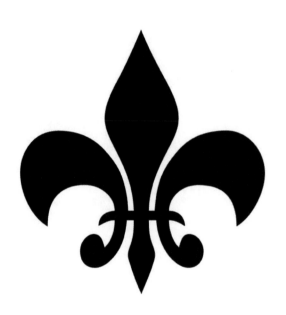

Polygraphs

Polygraphs. Don't you love them? A machine that can detect if a person is lying or not. What a joke. Ever heard of Hollywood? Home of the best actors in the world, meaning best liars in the world. Acting is like lying, you say and act a complete fabrication. Any good liar can pass a polygraph. And don't you love it when a suspect or an accused fails a polygraph? The prosecution loves to publicize that. When the suspect or accused passes a polygraph, the prosecution always brings up what we all say; that anyone can pass it and that it's inadmissible in court. Cut the crap.

My Favorites today

Robin Meade. Don't we love her? Fabulous teeth. I love and watch HLN every morning. The best way to deliver the news—very simple, fun, and casual.

My favorite film stars? Al Pacino, Anthony Hopkins, Denzel Washington, George Clooney, Brad Pitt, Morgan Freeman, Daniel Craig, Cate Blanchette, Kate Winslet, Angela Bassett, Angelina Jolie, and Dakota Fanning in film. TV? Charles Barkley, Steven A. Smith, Michael Wilbon, Howard Stern, and Robin Meade.

My favorite artists? Koffi Olomide, Anita Baker, Marvin Gaye, Whitney Houston, Chaka Khan, Mary J Blige, Joe, and, of course, Adele.

My favorite shows ever? The Blacklist, Blind Spot, The Affair, The Six Million Dollar Man, Gilligan's Island, The Jeffersons, and Laurel and Hardy.

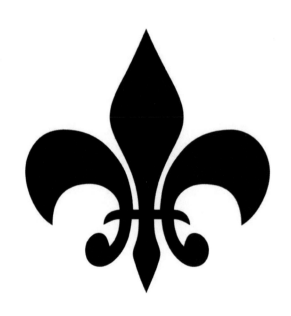

9/11

I love you, Bill Clinton. The best U.S. president ever, and I'm rooting for Hillary Clinton for the next president of the United States. However, you dropped the ball. You dropped the ball big time during your administration. The World Trade Center was attacked before 9/11. A bomb went off and there was loss of life, not like 9/11, but people died. Those people weren't respected and that attack wasn't taken seriously. It was orchestrated by Osama bin laden.

We did not see or get any kind of hype and determination like on 9/11 to go and get bin Laden. When 9/11 occurred, we saw the hype, the planes, jets, and ships getting ready. There was so much energy to go and get him. No money would be too much for the operation to get him. The U.S. was relentless to find Osama bin Laden. Too bad it took 9/11, which was unthinkable, the Towers coming down, and so much loss of life. It should have started, this focus and determination and relentless manhunt, when the World Trade Center was attacked with a bomb and there "were only minimal casualties." Minimal? No life is minimal. You should've gone after him long before 9/11.

I watched Colin Powell and Rudy Giuliani on TV speak about the attacks, on 9/12 or 13—I can't remember the exact day. Colin Powell said the terrorists failed. He said the terrorists tried to kill the American Spirit and destroy democracy and they failed. Well, that's true if that's what they tried to do, but they did not try to kill the American Spirit and destroy democracy. They tried to knock down the Towers, and they SUCCEEDED, Colin Powell. They tried to train in the U.S. (pilots), and they SUCCEEDED. They tried to sneak through airport security and SUCCEEDED. They tried to hijack planes, and they SUCCEEDED. They tried to knock down the Towers, and they SUCCEEDED. They tried to kill American lives, and they SUCCEEDED.

Why was I at work 9/12 reading the paper on my break and crying? Because they SUCCEEDED. Never sugar coat reality. A real leader or coach accepts what's happened and takes action. You don't go into denial. Can you imagine being a football player and losing 21-0 and your coach telling you that the other team didn't win? Absolutely not!

No they didn't succeed in killing the American Spirit or democracy, but yes, they SUCCEEDED in almost 90% of their plan, which included knocking down the Towers and killing Americans.

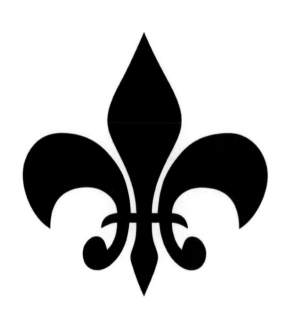

Mayor Rudy Giuliani

Rudy Giuliani Time Person of the Year??? Please. Every single mayor in every city in America would have done what Giuliani did.

Rudy Giuliani did nothing above and beyond what any other mayor would've done, absolutely nothing that another mayor would not had.

The real Time Person of the Year (for that year) is the entire group of fire department, police department, and medical personnel in New York that did what they did during that whole tragedy—not Rudy Giuliani. Not saying he should've suited up as a fireman and tried to put fires out or rescue people, but had he done that, it would've been super, super, super cool.

I simply cannot imagine another mayor doing anything less than what Giuliani did. I can't. Hats off, respect, and all praises due to the FDNY. I can't thank you enough. Adding insult to injury, Giuliani later tried to exploit this and run for the Oval Office. Pffff.

The Paris attacks

I don't get it. I do sympathize with the French people and government for the loss of life from the ISIS attacks on November 13, 2015. However, the response puzzles me. I saw on TV French military jets being deployed with all determination and focus to hunt down the perpetrators who were ISIS. I saw on TV that these jets had bombed and destroyed ISIS targets in Syria. Wait a minute, how come you didn't do that November 12, 2015, or any time before that? ISIS has been a menace for a while now— killing British and American journalists who are your friends, France. So why wait to destroy or attack these targets in Syria after the attacks on Paris? Unless you, the French, were already bombing and destroying their targets in Syria and it wasn't publicized, and I pray you were. Don't have this determination to destroy ISIS simply because of the Paris attacks. No, ISIS is a threat to everyone and you should, anybody, have a focus and determination to destroy it regardless of who they attack next.

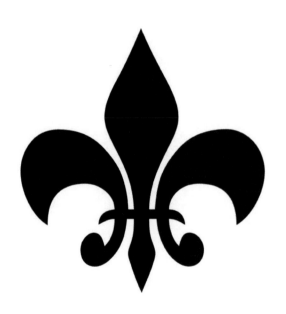

Prisons and education

I saw a post on Facebook showing stats of how much the U.S. spends on prisons and education versus other countries. The post was blasting the U.S. for spending so much on prisons and the penal system.

Well, guess what? If you steal, you're going to jail. If you molest my two-year-old daughter, you're going to jail. If you kill somebody, foolishly, over them stepping on your brand new Jordans, you're going to jail. If you rape somebody on campus, you're going to jail. If you kill somebody in the hood over some drugs, you're going to jail. All of these situations are the ills of America today.

Don't expect to get a party thrown if you commit any of these acts or to get a scholarship to NYU. No, you're going to jail, buddy. You're going to jail, sweetheart. If a lot of people are committing these acts, a lot of them are going to jail. Therefore, a lot of money will be spent to build prisons and money for incarceration. Don't blame the government. Don't do all this analysis on how much this or how much that. Don't steal, don't rape, don't molest, don't kill, don't embezzle, don't do the crime and you won't do the time! For the person who put up the post, I want to see what they do when three dudes home invade him and molest his daughter, rape his wife, beat him up, and then walk after a trial (no prison). That's right, I want to see that person repost that silly post on Facebook.

Actions have consequences, no matter the price you have to pay for your actions.

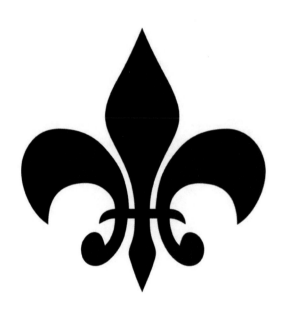

The rich lifestyle

The rich are rich. So what? Get over it. They worked hard for it or they inherited it. So what, leave them alone. People love to hate rich people. Pfff. Pathetic, how lame. People get surprised when they see a person driving a $500,000 car. If he wants to, his money, not yours; his life, not yours.

Would you, the lame people, say no if that same guy driving that $500K car tipped you $10,000? Or even a grand? You only like him when he does something for you, but not if he doesn't. So lame.

And remember this: the rich can gamble $1,000 a pop on a pool game, you can't. If you work at Wendy's and make $9 an hour and bet your buddy fifty bucks on a football game and lose, knowing you have two kids and make under $300 a week, you have lost more than Michael Jordan losing $1,000 on a pool game. He's worth over 500 million. He can lose $1,000 or $2,000 on a pool game, but you can't. You cannot lose fifty bucks at all on a football bet.

Stop criticizing and hating the rich and their possessions. They can afford it, get over it!

Blood and love

Blood doesn't mean anything to me, nothing at all. Love does. Enter the Menendez brothers. Two brothers who killed their parents execution style in the 90s. They made it seem like intruders or gangsters. After inheriting the money, they went on luxury shopping sprees buying Rolex watches and Porsches. They got busted. In court, they even went to the level of accusing their parents of child abuse? Even crying! You have to be kidding me. Talk about adding insult to injury. You kill me, and then you falsely accuse me of being an abuser? An RIT student recently took an ax to his parents—an ax! He drove at night from Rochester, New York to Albany, attacked them, and drove back in the early morning. Thruway cameras caught him, and his DNA was on the thruway ticket, too, along with the campus security footage showing him returning in the morning.

His father died, but his mom survived. What? Can you imagine surviving an ax to the face more than twenty times? She first said he did it and then recanted (out of love) saying it wasn't him. Everyday people kill their own, betray their own, hate their own, or take an ax to their own.

Blood doesn't mean anything to me, nothing at all. Love does, it's the ultimate. Love transcends everything. Love is beautiful.

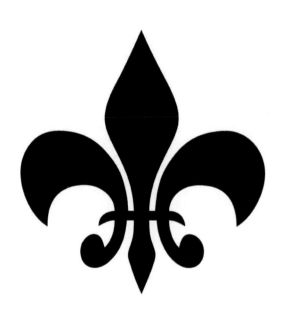

Comedy and insults

If I'm caught gossiping or calling you names, that's right, insulting you, it's bad and wrong. If I'm doing it on stage, it's ok, it's funny, and I even get a check for it. We call it comedy.

Yeah, right. I believe in comedy about situations, animals, or about myself. Not others. Never. I don't care how you twist it and say it's just a joke. So many people run under the umbrella of comedy to go at somebody. Bull crap. I used to believe in comedy like that and jokes about people. Not anymore. I took a long time and just thought about it. Why, if I'm angry at that white person, can I call him racist names and it's wrong, but I can get on stage and twist and arrange everything nicely and still call him these racist names and it becomes comedy? No. I don't believe in that. Joke about animals, everyday social or human situations, or about yourself, but targeting a specific person or race is not cool to me just because you're on stage. Get the hell outta here! Simply my opinion.

A beautiful woman

As a man, I've been guilty of this too, in the past though. It's not right. Every woman in the world deserves extra help or assistance for anything.

Not just because she's beautiful. Put a hidden camera in public somewhere and see how a beautiful woman is treated compared to an obese or poor woman. Nothing wrong with admiring or looking at a beautiful woman longer than an average looking woman or an obese or poor one, but helping, assisting, and only being nice to the beautiful one is wrong!

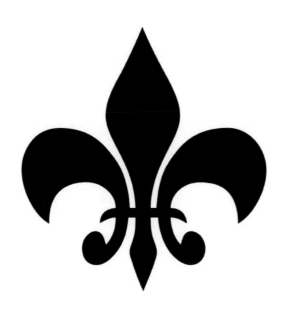

Criticizing Valentine's Day

Valentine's Day—a lot of people love it, a lot of people hate it. It's been dubbed the Hallmark Holiday. Valentine's Day really gets a bad rap from the people that I know personally. People say that every day is Valentine's Day, and that it's silly, and that it's just a fabricated Holiday for money (selling cards).

I disagree. I love Valentine's Day. Valentine's Day is absolutely no different than Mother's Day or Father's Day. Every day is also Mother's Day...that's for the critics; every day should also be Father's Day. Where is the crime in choosing a certain day to celebrate or honor a love for someone? Where is the crime? Of course you can also choose to make it "everyday" as the critics love to suggest. How can anyone truly hate or criticize Valentine's Day, yet like and celebrate Mother's Day and Father's Day? It doesn't make sense to me. What makes sense to me is someone hating all three and disagrees with all three. There it makes sense. I disagree with that person, but I respect and appreciate his or her stance. That person is not contradicting him- or herself. I can express my gratitude and my love for Mom every day, year-round, why just in May? That's for the critics, and it's those same critics who still buy the cards, candy, dinner, and a gift. Why? Scared he or she might leave you? Stick to your opinion and don't partake, it's as simple as that.

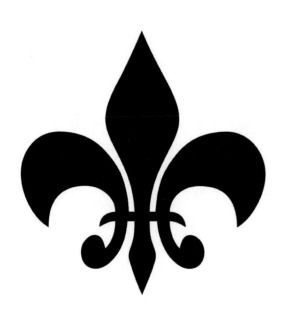

The other ill

Racism is a serious cancer in society and will never go away. It will always be around, forever. There's another ill that people don't talk about as much but is just as bad as racism. It's called "classicism" (my own word). The mistreatment of people because of their background or financial class.

Inner city people around the globe are treated like dirt, like garbage compared to rich people. Meaning, all white, black, Hispanic, and all other races in the city who are middle-class down to poor are nothing compared to the rich in society. The rich, meaning the rich not white people as some may assume. I was at a FedEx once and stood in line for like ten minutes. I was third in line. The guy behind the counter never said "hi," or "I'll be right with you," or anything to me at all.

A white woman comes in, gets in line behind and immediately this dude—a black guy, too—says so nicely to her, "Hello, ma'am, we'll be right with you." Unbelievable! I went to the store manager and told him the case and told the guy, too! Right on the spot, I stand in line for ten minutes without acknowledgement and a white woman walks in, and just like that she's greeted and acknowledged? The store manager apologized, but I would've let that employee go. You absolutely do not treat people like that.

Just like at Kaufmann's (now Macy's)—yes I'm naming names. My son was a year old, and I walk into the toddler section for clothes. I was looking for the best Tommy Hilfiger they had because at the time that's all I was wearing. For twenty minutes I was browsing and browsing, looking and looking while a group of three or four employees, all women, just stood there chatting and never offered me any assistance whatsoever, none. For twenty minutes! The next day I went in to see the store manager, because I used to spend a lot of money at Kaufman's. As a responsible adult and citizen, you have to report employees who mistreat customers like that. When the store manager came down to see me, guess what? That's right, she happened to be among the women who had completely ignored me, a man shopping for baby clothes. Every man needs help when shopping for baby clothes.

I was disgusted, couldn't believe it. I went above her and saw the district manager. Don't treat people like that. If they recognized me as this real rich, famous person, they would've assisted me ten times out of ten, but I was just average looking so it was "screw him." They also could've been racist. Bottom line is, if I were a star, rich and famous, of any race they would have assisted me. I looked average, so they threw me in the category of city people, who are always connected with the poor.

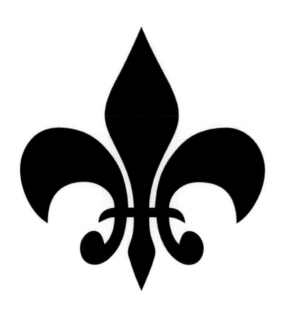

The University of Notre Dame

The University of Notre Dame had a big scandal going on. They went out and got a black coach for their football team. To distract us. It was a first. His name was Ty Willingham. After three years, Ty Willingham was fired. Okay, no problem. Notre Dame brings in Charlie Weiss from the New England Patriots as the new coach. After three years, Charlie Weiss has a worse record then Ty Willingham but he gets a ten-year extension. What??? Are you kidding me??? Seriously??? I got nothing more to write.

Tickets

Professional sports are impossible to attend for a poor family of two or three and very hard for a middle-class family. Yet people just keep going and going to games. When does it stop? The ones responsible for these ticket prices are you—you the person or family who keeps going to the games. The owners and teams say, "Ah, don't worry. People love their favorite players. They'll keep coming, they're not staying home." I would like to take a very serious tone right now. I want to call the NFL and the NBA out right now. The dirt-poor kids at the playgrounds today are the backbone and the soul of the NBA and the NFL. It's not a secret that the majority of all NBA and NFL players are black and came from very hard times, to put it nicely. It's these same very poor kids who are the superstar players in the NBA and NFL, yet these kids at playgrounds today could never go to an NBA game or NFL game. These ticket prices just keep going and going because these owners and the NBA and the NFL don't care. They just know that you, yes you will keep going to the games and buying the $40 hot dogs and $50 sodas. Shame on you. These poor families that cannot attend a game ever are the reason these leagues flourish, that little black, dirt-poor kid at the playground is the LeBron James of tomorrow, the Odell Beckham of tomorrow, the Alex Rodriguez of tomorrow, but for now he cannot go to any games, even though he's among the superstars who make up these leagues.

The tackiest things

I used to go out on jobs, projects in construction, and come lunchtime I would offer to buy my co-workers lunch. Yet one day this one guy instead of just saying, "Nice of you, Guy, but, no thanks, I'm not hungry," he said, "I don't want a hot dog, buy me a black and mild instead." I asked, "What's a black & mild?" I thought it was some kind of sausage or something. No, it was those little cigars. Pfff. Are you serious? Just say, "No, thank you." I'm not your nicotine provider.

Another time I offer to take a female co-worker to lunch, my treat. I bought two lunches with drinks (sodas in a bottle). This chick didn't eat a quarter, or even a half a quarter, of her food. She takes a couple of bites and shuts her container, never opens her pop. I finish my food. She brings her food back to the job and puts it in the fridge along with her pop. Really? I'm not trying to supply you with groceries, just wanted to buy you lunch. What the hell is wrong with people? That's the epitome of tacky right there. She took it home for dinner.

And, don't you love it when you give somebody money to buy you something and there's considerable change and they don't give it back to you. Tacky. I'm not talking about the ones who forget, but the ones who deliberately keep your three or four dollars. Grow up, please.

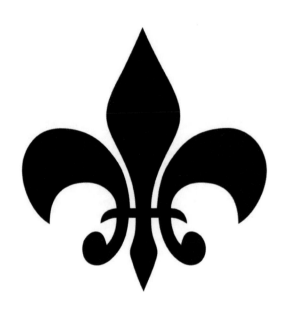

Using the bathroom

To be or not to be, or in this case, to look or not to look. Well, there's nothing to look at. People ask, "Do you look or not when you flush after a dump?" Let me see, when I use the bathroom, I drop my pants, do my thing, and flush right after. I spray if there's some spray, I chill (sitting), do my thing again, and flush. I spray again, still sitting. If I'm home I will browse a few pages of a magazine and keep the cycle going. When I've finished, I wipe and flush, and by the time I get up, whether I look or not, there's nothing to look at. I can't remember the last time I saw my own stuff. Why would I want to look?

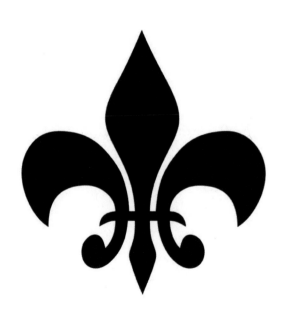

Obesity and poverty

How can a poor person be overweight? Seriously, I could never understand that fact. You have people who have been dirt-poor their entire lives, yet they are overweight. How in the world is that possible? American food must be very fattening and bad for you.

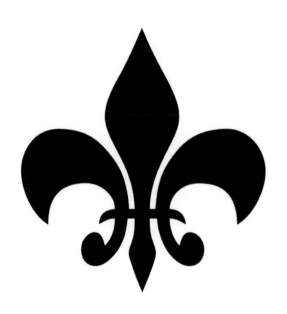

Gifts

Gifts, gifts, gifts. We all love them, everybody does. Gifts, I've come to understand, are really misinterpreted. In life we have needs, and we have wants. Enter, your children. Your children have needs, and they have wants. You, the parent, are responsible for your kids' needs. Food on the table, a coat in the winter, a toothbrush—those are needs your kid is due from you. No ifs, ands, or buts.

Today, sadly, some people—mostly the poor ones and the ignorant ones—have come to make needs as gifts. Not! You have to buy your kid a coat for winter. You have to buy your kid clothes if he or she doesn't have any. Those aren't gifts. No. If he or she already has enough good clothes, and you want to add some real cool ones (Polo, Gap, Nike, etc.), then yes, those are gifts. You got parents who don't take care of their kids. They smoke and drink all of the kid's money (child support or DSS). Kids will be naked all year and then at Christmas they go buy them clothes and call them gifts. Really? Are you kidding? That's not a gift. That's a need that they've been due all year that you smoked and drank all year just to trick them at the end of the year that it's a gift. If you have to buy something anyway (a need), it's not a gift.

An Xbox is a gift, a necklace for your daughter is a gift, $200 Jordans are a gift because your kids do not need these items, they want them. Get it right, folks.

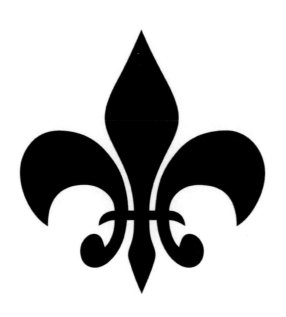

We, human beings

The human spirit, at times is very loving, merciful, and very giving. At times, it can be a monster, evil, demonic. It's very troubling, perplexing, and fascinating just how the contrast can be.

The human being is responsible for some of the greatest marvels on the planet. The television, telephone, radio, automobile, the computer, along with the Internet and social media, are some of the greatest technological marvels ever. The human being has gone to the moon. The human being has made medicine to heal. The human being is also not just tech savvy, but loving, merciful, and generous to those in need, those hurting, and those needing help. There are a lot of humanitarians—religious ones and regular ones—all over the world. Oprah Winfrey, amongst others, are humanitarians with very giving spirits.

On the other hand, the human being can also have the most horrific spirit. When I look at what certain people do to each other, I say, "Wow." What a contrast to the humanitarian spirit I was just talking about. People who kill their own parents for money, people who rape their own children, people who beat their own siblings as if they were slaves in Egypt, people who take an ax to their parents for money, or people who tie a man to a chain and hook it behind a truck and drive off and drag him to his death simply because he's black. This is unbelievable to me. The human spirit and human beings are very complex, from the good they do to the bad.

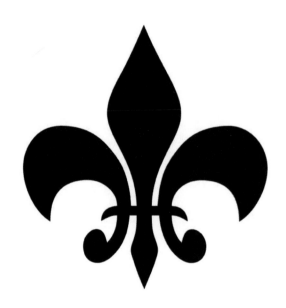

I love New York

New York. I love New York. New York, in my opinion, is the best state in America, with the best city in America, the best city in the world, New York City.

I grew up in New York State. It has all I love and all I need. All four seasons. I love all four. I love changing my wardrobe season to season. Who wants ninety degrees year-round? Who wants ninety degrees at seven am? Who wants floods, tornadoes, and hurricanes? Which are not a laughing matter at all.

So much in America started in New York State. Whether literature or technology, New York has it all. All across the state.

I love the fact that almost everybody coming to America has to come through New York. New York is like the gate. Having lived in Albany, Brooklyn, and Rochester, it's great to have gotten three angles of the great state, downstate, the capital, and upstate. Why else would a leader, born in Chicago, Illinois, and a former First Lady of Arkansas want to be senator of New York State? (Hillary Clinton.)

What about the famous people born in New York State? Al Pacino (my favorite actor of all time); Robert De Niro; Robert Downey, Jr.; Sylvester Stallone; Anne Hathaway; Scarlett Johansson; Tea Leoni; Rosario Dawson; Marisa Tomei; Jack Nicholson; JJ Abrams; and so many more.

I love the history of New York, meaning New York State history. It's good for our kids to not have to travel far to see what they study and learn in class. Growing up in Albany, I used to love going on field trips at the Empire State Plaza. Going to the museums there and seeing New York State history right there during school hours. It was absolutely great. Whether in film, music, or sports, New York State has produced the best of the best, hands down. It's not even close if we had to compare. It's not even a contest. From Martin Scorsese, to Mariah Carey, to Jay-Z, to Michael Jordan, yes, Michael was in Brooklyn, New York! I love it. To Carmelo Anthony.

I love the fact that there are so many professional sports franchises in New York State. The Giants, the Jets, the Bills, the Rangers, the Islanders, the Sabres, the Yankees, the Mets, the Knicks, and the Nets. Can't forget the Syracuse Orangemen or St. John's Red Storm. Did I mention that one of the most prestigious events in sports in the world is played annually in New York State? The U.S. Open, one of the four Grand Slams in tennis, Flushing Meadows, Queens, New York. So, whether I want to go to a great ball game in Orchard Park or at the Carrier Dome or in the Bronx; go to a great university in the U of R, SU, or NYU; dine at some of the finest restaurants in the country; check out some great theater; go to a great museum; or shop at J.M. Weston's (luxury French shoemaker); the only store in the entire U.S.; or check out the ever so evolving New York Fashion Week, I can do it all here, in New York State.

California and Texas, even Florida, have multiple big cities. New York State? Only one, and that's New York City, yet we're still the best state in the country, in my opinion.

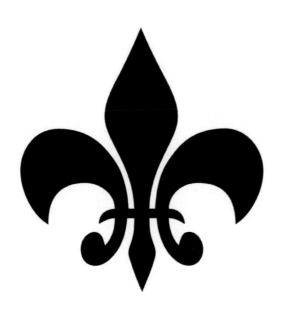

Determination

Determination, firmness of purpose. I watched Tererai Trent on Oprah in 2011. Instantly she became one of my favorite people ever. She is more than a heroine. She is a true inspiration.

Tererai Trent, born in Zimbabwe, was forbidden from going to school, forced into marriage, had three kids by the age of eighteen, and suffered tremendous emotional and physical abuse from her husband. Yet she had a dream, and she achieved it. Her dream was coming to America and getting a PhD. Wow.

Barack Obama, a young black guy from Chicago with a funny last name, born in Hawaii of a Kenyan father and an American mother. Doesn't sound like somebody about to run for the Oval Office, yet he did, and he won—twice.

These two people are the epitome of Determination, with a capital D. They pursued their dreams with unflinching determination.

For years and years, I neglected my dream of becoming a writer, an author. I met a guy a year ago with a great life. Married, two kids, two homes, and a good job. He wanted to "help" me get ahead in life by joining him and doing what he did. He went on explaining everything about his job. Then I told him, "No, I want to become a writer."

He paused for like two minutes, he never said a word, and looked at me like a total idiot, like I was dreaming. Then he continued explaining to me his job and how to get started. He never asked if I had any contacts or connections in publishing, he never asked what I wanted to write about. Zip, zero, nothing, nada, absolutely nothing. I felt like an idiot. I felt so insulted. I felt so dejected.

At the time, I had no contacts or connections in the business. I hadn't even written one word or one syllable of this book. Less than a year after my conversation with that guy, I wrote my first book. Exactly six months later.

Exactly one year after my conversation with him, my book is finished and in production. I'm a published writer. I'm not a great one. I'm not Steven King. You can't even put me in a conversation with names like that, but I've achieved my goal, and my dream is unfolding. I look at the two people I just talked about, Dr. Tererai Trent and President Barack Obama, and I see one word, Determination. Thank you to my fifth and sixth grade Principal Sister Johanne, for noticing me back then and telling me, "one day you're going to be a writer."

57998123R00113

Made in the USA
Charleston, SC
30 June 2016